To: Bill Campbell
    for his Birthday
                1983.

    from the Collins'

SOUTH PACIFIC BREWERY

THE FIRST THIRTY YEARS

SOUTH

PACIFIC BREWERY

THE FIRST THIRTY YEARS

James Sinclair

Robert Brown & Associates

Designed & published by
Robert Brown & Associates (Aust.) Pty. Ltd.
P.O. Box 29,
Bathurst, N.S.W. 2795 Australia

© James Sinclair 1983

National Library of Australia
Cataloguing-in-Publication data

Sinclair, James, 1928-
  South Pacific Brewery

  Includes index
  ISBN 0 909197 36 9

  1. South Pacific Brewery — History
  2. Brewing industries — Papua New Guinea — History. I. Title.

338.7'6633'09953

Printed in Hong Kong

Contents

William Henry Johns, O.B.E.,
1912-1982.

Preface

This book is dedicated to William Henry Johns, General Manager of South Pacific Brewery Limited from 1957 to 1973.

Bill Johns came to New Guinea as a young man of twenty-one in the early 1930s to work on the goldfields at Edie Creek, where he was married in 1939 to Heather Lesley. When war broke out, Bill stayed behind and joined ANGAU, serving in Papua New Guinea throughout the war. After the war Bill was commissioned by the Commonwealth Government of Australia to start up trading along the coast of Papua.

From 1952 to 1957, Bill was General Manager of P.M.F. and became General Manager of South Pacific Brewery Limited in 1957.

Bill was a great family man and cherished his forty-two years living in Papua New Guinea. After his family, Bill loved his SP Lager and his golf.

Bill was a man of action and steered South Pacific Brewery through its formative years. Bill was a leader in the community. He worked voluntarily for both the Australian Administration and the Independent Government of Papua New Guinea as a member of the Papua New Guinea Electricity Commission, and Chairman of the Papua New Guinea Investment Corporation. He was a member of the Executive of the Employer's Federation of Papua New Guinea, President of the Port Moresby Chamber of Commerce and Chairman of the South Pacific Games Trust Fundraising Committee.

His great forté was training which he pursued very successfully in all his endeavours.

In this book there are many characters that have worked and played in Papua New Guinea, but none better known or more respected than the 'Brewery Bill'.

Bruce A. Flynn, O.B.E.

Foreword

This is the story of the first thirty years of a brewing company that began during the Australian colonial era in Papua New Guinea.

South Pacific Brewery was formed to produce beer to satisfy the thirsts of Australian colonialists, at a time when Papua New Guineans were forbidden to drink beer by law.

The Brewery continues to produce high quality beer in a Papua New Guinea that is today an independent State.

I am grateful to many people for assistance in gathering material for this book, in particular the late Bill Johns, Bruce Flynn, Jim Cromie, Lloyd Hurrell, Ken Webb, Ron Corden, Roy McKain, Rudi Bertram, Bertie Heath, Gerry Faramus and other staff members, past and present, of South Pacific Brewery Limited.

My thanks are also due to Mrs J. M. Bourke, P. A. Yeomans, and Wayne Grant, Managing Editor of the Papua New Guinea *Post-Courier* newspaper.

James Sinclair

Presentation of the Gold Medal Award for winning the International Lager Competition in Birmingham, United Kingdom, 1980. Left to right: Leka Wari and Patrick Francis, SP Brewers, with Brian Morris, Corporate Promotions Manager, Industrial Trade Fairs.

Introduction

It is a great pleasure to introduce this history of South Pacific Brewery Limited, written by my old friend, James Sinclair.

For this is more than a narrow company history. It is also a sociological study that will be required reading for students of modern Papua New Guinea history, and for all who are interested in the welfare of our people.

The position of a Brewing Company in an evolving society such as ours is obviously a delicate one. I congratulate the Management of South Pacific Brewery on outlining the problems, as well as the benefits, that have resulted from the introduction of liquor to the people of Papua New Guinea.

Boyamo Sali, C.M.G., M.P.
Minister for Media

The first hotel erected in Port Moresby, The Moresby Hotel, was built around 1892 on the site of today's 'bottom pub'.

Joe Bourke.

1

Joe Bourke Builds a Pub

In November, 1947, a brief notice in the Papua and New Guinea *Government Gazette* advised Territorians that one Joseph Michael Bourke had applied for a liquor licence for premises he proposed to erect in the town of Wau, to be called the Kaindi Hotel. The licence was approved in December, and Bourke was allowed eight months in which to complete his hotel.

With characteristic vigour, Joe Bourke began his task, watched with warm approval by the drinkers of the little Morobe goldfields town — of which there were many. He built in fragrant pine, cut from the abundant stands that clothed in soft green the flanks of the serene Wau Valley, and he made rapid progress. In a few short months the little hotel, homely, but comfortable enough, was nearing completion.

Joe Bourke was one of the pioneers of the Morobe Goldfield. He came from a pioneer family, too. His grandfather, John Bourke, arrived in Australia from Tipperary, Ireland, in 1834. He was one of the defenders of the Eureka Stockade, and in 1838 carried the first parcel of mails from Melbourne to the Murray River.

Joe Bourke was born in January, 1899, in the North Queensland town of Ayr. He came to what was then the Mandated Territory of New Guinea in 1925, as a plantation overseer for the Expropriation Board, formed after the Great War to take over and manage plantations once owned by German settlers. Strong and active, Bourke liked the outdoor life of a plantation overseer, but this was too narrow an occupation to satisfy a man of his character for long. His chance soon came.

Around about 1922 a legendary prospector, William 'Shark-Eye' Park, found gold on Koranga Creek, a tributary of the Bulolo River in the Morobe District. So remote was the location that the news of the find did not leak out for a long time, but soon Territorians in the know were exchanging increasingly taller stories of gold coming out of the Koranga in cigarette tins, hat boxes and finally buckets.

Then came the find that was to fire the imagination of the mining world and which directly led to the development of Bulolo Gold Dredging Limited and the enrichment of the Mandated Territory economy. In January, 1926, prospectors Bill Royal and Dick Glasson discovered gold at Edie Creek. Values were utterly fabulous, far greater than anything previously discovered in PNG, and a 'rush' of extraordinary dimensions followed. Men flocked to the Edie from the furthermost corners of the world. Some found their fortune; most did not. But over the next few years aerial transport came to the Morobe Goldfield; the towns of Wau, Bulolo, Lae and Salamaua developed; the dredges began to tear up the gravelled flats of the Bulolo Valley, and gold became the principal export of the Mandated Territory.

Joe Bourke saw the whole thing. Early in 1926 he was offered, and accepted a position as policeman on the Morobe field, at an annual salary of £366. 'I had no idea whatever of the duties of a policeman', he wrote in an unpublished account, years later, 'but this was right up my alley. The job had all the hallmarks of adventure. The only qualification necessary was physical fitness, because of the primitive conditions on the Goldfield. I reported to Major Stanley Stanmore Skeete, ex-Army, District Officer and deputy of the Administrator at Salamaua. "Go to the Police Barracks," he said, "and select five policeboys, then on to the Native Labour Compound and get yourself fifteen carriers, ask the Storeman for sufficient rations for twenty days, pick up the Edie Creek mail, get a pinnace out to Busama, take the Buang track to Edie Creek, and report there to Ward Oakley"'.

Six days later, a thoroughly exhausted Joe Bourke led his little band to Edie Creek, and the headquarters of Mining Warden Ward Oakley, senior representative of the Administration — a canvas fly stretched over bush saplings, with a desk composed of two upended patrol boxes. On the track from the beach Bourke had seen only one European, a dainty young woman

A dredger weighing over two thousand tonnes, which was flown into Bulolo piece by piece.

The settlement of Edie Creek.

called Doris Booth — first white woman on the field — who was mining gold on the Bulolo River at a place she and her husband called *Cliffside*.

It was bitterly cold at Edie Creek, 1 980 metres above sea level. 'You'd better find yourself a place to pitch camp,' said Ward Oakley. Bourke found a tiny flat piece of ground near a small creek, and there he built the first Police Post on the Edie. 'Little did I know that I had pitched my tent on one of the richest spots on the field', he wrote. 'It was later known as the El Dorado, and it eventually produced £250,000-worth of gold'.

Such riches were not for Policemaster Bourke, although he sometimes took a hand in the heavy poker games played by successful miners, where a thousand pounds, and more, often changed ownership in a single night. Joe Bourke was a life-long poker player, and a good one. One needed skill — and nerve — to compete when games commenced at one pound blind, two pounds for cards, with the sky as the limit. But more often Bourke was in

3

Above *A Government patrol trekking through* kunai *country.*

the bush with his policeboys, patrolling the Salamaua Track and protecting the carriers who toiled in their thousands over those high, harsh mountains to keep the mining camps supplied. Attacks on the carrier-lines by the warrior tribes of the mountains were all too frequent, and many a carrier was killed and eaten on the Salamaua Track. It was not until the introduction of Junkers aircraft in 1928 by the pioneer aviation company, Guinea Airways Limited, that the day of the carrier was over.

In November, 1926, Joe Bourke was escorting a Government carrier-line through the open *kunai* country of the Upper Bulolo Valley when they came across the beheaded, blood-spattered corpses of two carriers, half hidden in the long grass. On reporting the slaughter, Bourke was ordered to proceed forthwith to the Upper Bulolo and there locate and arrest the killers. Near the heavily stockaded village of Kaisenik, one of a number of Biangai tribe villages in the region, Bourke and his little party of five police were joined by 'Blue' Nickols, Patrol Officer, and his police, and together they succeeded after a fierce battle in arresting twenty warriors, including Lason, a famous fighter. Then they set off for Salamaua, with their prisoners.

Salamaua, when they arrived there, was almost deserted. The little Burns Philp steamer, *Marsina*, was in port, and in traditional Territory fashion the thirsty residents of Salamaua were on board, drinking iced draught beer as fast as they could in the tiny bar. Bourke and Nickols hastened to join them — such rare opportunities were not to be missed!

Later, Lason and seventeen of his warriors escaped from the flimsy Salamaua gaol and returned to the business of butchering carriers. To Lason and his men, these carriers — recruited from the coast — were strangers, and just as much the enemy as the white miners now occupying the tribal lands of the Biangai in ever-increasing numbers. Lason's band, and fighters from other Biangai villages, increased their attacks on the carrier-lines.

Below *Kukukuku tribesmen at the Benir headwaters.*

A Guinea Airways Limited Junkers aircraft.

In the end, the unfortunate Biangai warriors had to lose their war against the white man. The rapidly developing gold industry was too important to be hindered by the activities of what the authorities considered to be a bunch of savages. The carriers were becoming so terrified of the dangers of the Salamaua Track that they began to refuse their loads; supplies started to run out on the goldfield. J.D.McLean was appointed Mining Warden, and he decided to stop the Biangai raids once and for all. In a short, hard campaign, government forces, aided by the angry white miners, defeated the Biangai people in a series of fights, and burned their principal village, Kaisenik. Joe Bourke was in the thick of the action, with his armed police. He had several narrow escapes from Biangai arrows.

Peace now reigned on the Morobe Goldfield, and Bourke quickly became bored. Towards the end of 1927 he resigned his position and became a goldminer. He pegged a claim on Midas Creek, a feeder of the Edie and in the very first day of working he washed up sixty ounces of gold! 'All I knew of alluvial mining I gained from looking over the shoulders of the chaps with the knowhow', Bourke later wrote. 'But, believe me, the gold bug really bites when your first dish shows this fascinating metal glittering in the sun. I contracted gold fever in 1927, and it's been with me more or less ever since'. He soon developed into a skilled miner and prospector.

Joe prospered, modestly. The aeroplane transformed the Morobe Goldfield; world airfreighting records were established and broken during the early 1930s. Wau, Bulolo, Lae and Salamaua grew into respectable towns, with shops, schools, churches, libraries, a picture theatre, clubs and hotels. And as life on the once-primitive Morobe Goldfield became easier, more comfortable, and dull, so Joe Bourke once again grew restless.

In mid-1934 Bourke went to Sydney for a holiday, and there he met an old friend also down on leave, the prospector and mining engineer, Tom Yeomans. Yeomans, noted throughout New Guinea as a bushman, had

Miner, Tom Yeomans, lends a hand as the first Kukukuku ever to take an aeroplane trip is persuaded to look into the cabin of a DH50, piloted by Tommy O'Dea, 1933.

been employed by Bulolo Gold Dredging Ltd. since 1928 to seek out new mineral deposits in the farthest corners of the land. It was Tom Yeomans who laid out the original camp for BGD Ltd., and who constructed the first aerodrome. He was the kind of man who could turn his hand to anything, a good mate whose word was his bond.

'Joe,' said Yeomans, 'How'd you like to get back into the bush? You must be tired of sitting down at Wau. How about a prospecting trip around the headwaters of the Fly and the Sepik?'

This was virtually unknown country in 1934. Only two white men had walked there: Charles Karius, Resident Magistrate of the Papuan Service, and Ivan Champion, Patrol Officer, during their great North-West Patrol of 1927-28. A prospecting journey through this virgin territory was an exciting thought. 'It was a bright, shining beacon to the gold prospector', Bourke wrote. He immediately accepted Yeoman's offer, made on behalf of the big English mining company, Oroville Dredging Co. Ltd.

Space does not permit a proper description of Joe Bourke's wanderings over the next two years — this would require another book. The Oroville gold expedition, the most ambitious ever launched in PNG, was led by a remarkable American mining engineer, J. Ward Williams. During the course of the expedition, from 1935 to 1937, Ward Williams and his men — they included Bourke and W.T.Korn, prospectors; Stuart Campbell and Ken Garden, pilots; Tom Park, George Andersen, Jack Gwilt and Wallace Kienzle — located and built basecamps and aerodromes at Kiunga, on the Fly River, and Telefomin, on the Sepik Headwaters, and explored and prospected the Fly, Alice, Strickland and Sepik headwaters. Bourke, Korn and Kienzle examined thousands of square miles of unexplored country during these years, travelling on foot through some of the most difficult terrain in PNG. They found nothing. They prospected the streams and mountains running through to the Dutch New Guinea border and finally established a camp on the May River where the two prospectors drove a series of shafts, in one last attempt to prove the existence of payable gold. It was all in vain. Despite this prodigal outpouring of time, human effort and cold cash, the Ward Williams expedition did not find payable gold. Ward Williams admitted defeat, and went back to America.

By the time Joe Bourke returned to Wau at the end of 1937 the world scene was rapidly deteriorating, and war seemed certain. During the Great War, Bourke had served with 102 Howitzer Battery, from 1917 to 1919, and when the New Guinea Volunteer Rifles (NGVR) was formed, in September 1939, he immediately joined the Wau detachment.

War broke out in Europe, and in December, 1941, the Japanese attacked Pearl Harbour. In January and February, 1942, they invaded New Guinea, in overwhelming force. In shocking succession the principal coastal towns were bombed, destroyed and captured. Rabaul, Kokopo, Wewak, Kavieng, Namatanai, Madang, Lae and Salamaua fell, and the Japanese were masters of most of the Territory of New Guinea, and part of Papua. When they tried to capture the bastion of Port Moresby, vital to their over-all plans, the hitherto invincible Japanese were turned back for the first time on land in the Pacific war, and by numerically inferior Australian forces. They failed, too, to capture Wau, which would have served as a stepping-stone for another attempt on Port Moresby, although the town was badly damaged in the fighting.

The handful of men in the NGVR — the total approved strength of this force was only twenty officers and 400 men — were in no position to halt the Japanese onrush, but they fought bravely in many theatres, as scouts and in guerilla actions in support of AIF formations, particularly in the unit known as Kanga Force, formed in May, 1942, to harass the Japanese at Lae and Salamaua, and based at Wau.

With Joe Bourke in the NGVR were three other men of particular importance to this story; William Henry Johns, Thomas Zoffman and James Irwin Cromie. The NGVR was disbanded in 1942, most of its members being absorbed into ANGAU, the Australian New Guinea Administrative Unit. Joe Bourke was one of these, serving until late 1943, and for the rest of the war in small ships.

When civil administration was restored in PNG, Joe Bourke and his wife, Anna — who was always known as 'Billie', after the well-known American actress — settled in Lae, and then returned to Wau. Life in PNG in 1946 was spartan. The bitter tide of war had washed over much of the Morobe District. The Lae of yesteryear was gone, totally destroyed in the fighting. The town was now little more than the remains of a giant military encampment, and it was from this litter of war that the new Lae arose, phoenix-like. Salamaua, pre-war headquarters of the Morobe District, never grew again. Bulolo had been partially destroyed by Australian forces, to deny the marvellous equipment and workshop facilities of BGD Ltd. to the invaders. Wau had been shelled and bombed so heavily that few buildings still stood.

Civilians were slow to return to PNG after the war. They were regarded as a nuisance by the military authorities — it was not until 23 June, 1946, that civil administration was restored on the Gazelle Peninsula, the last remaining region under military control. The first sizeable contingent of Territorians, 160 in all, returned on the M.V.*Ormiston* in April, 1946, and this ship was under military direction. Most of these people had been clamouring for months for the right to return.

Returning residents re-established themselves as best they could, and usually resumed their old occupations. They were helped by generous war damage payments by the Australian Government, and by sales of war-surplus supplies and equipment, where jeeps in going condition could be purchased for as little as twenty pounds, and big ex-US Army White and Dodge trucks for one hundred. But there were material shortages of every kind. The basic necessities of life were in desperately limited supply. 'Miserable Rabaul!' mourned an article in the journal, *Pacific Islands Monthly* in October, 1946, bewailing the serious shortage of food in the town. A public meeting was convened to consider ways and means of obtaining supplies. 'Lae Goes on a Meat Bender!', went another report of the arrival of a rare, small shipment of frozen foods. 'No one actually goes hungry in Lae, but canned food is deadly monotonous...there are no matches, tobacco, sugar, and NO BEER! Lae today is fit only for people with a gift for making silk purses out of sow's ears...'.
'Madang is at the End of the Line', another correspondent wrote in despair. It was the same all over PNG. It was not until the early 1950s that the position markedly improved.

It was during these days of privation following the war that Joe Bourke got the idea of building a hotel in Wau. One of the most serious shortages in Territory towns was accommodation. Residents took over ex-military buildings and turned them into temporary houses, but there was no public accommodation; every hotel, residential club and boarding house on the New Guinea side had been destroyed.

In Lae, the redoubtable Mrs Flora Stewart was already at work to satisfy this urgent need. The first white woman to return to Lae after the war, she was a hotelier of great renown in the Morobe District. Born in Scotland in 1886, Flo Stewart first came to Papua in 1910 with her then husband, Harry Gofton, who was killed in the Great War. She took over the management of the Samarai Hotel in 1927, and in 1929 married Jim Stewart and purchased the original Wau Hotel from Harry Darby, calling it Hotel Bulolo. Her Hotel Cecil opened at Lae in February, 1936, on a site at Voco Point, near the waterfront. She named it in honour of the man who was primarily responsible for the formation of Bulolo Gold Dredging Ltd, and the introduction of aerial transport to the Goldfield; Cecil John Levien. She advertised the Cecil as being 'The Most Up-to-Date in the Islands! There are no less than four Plunge Baths and Showers, Electric Light, Fans and Septic tanks'.

Mrs Flora Stewart at Wau.

8

Neither the Bulolo nor the Cecil survived the war. Returning to Lae, Flo Stewart was received with great relief by the War Disposals and Administration authorities, at their wits' end trying to find accommodation for the rush of ex-servicemen, government officers, businessmen and other transients who often arrived, unannounced, expecting to be looked after. Flo Stewart was given every assistance to take over the huge, sprawling assemblage of tents and buildings which had comprised the AWAS (Australian Women's Army Service) Camp, a few miles out of town. This she turned into a hotel. She offered her guests 'any number' of well-furnished single rooms, and no less than fifty bathrooms with showers, plus hot water and laundry facilities. Her daughter, Miss Ela Gofton, assisted her in the task of management. The liquor licence formerly held for the old Hotel Cecil was transferred to the new establishment, also known (informally) as the Cecil.

The ex-AWAS Camp made a pretty dreadful hotel. Mrs Stewart found it almost as hard to obtain fresh foods and essentials as did the handful of white housewives in Lae, which by mid-1946 had a population of around 300 Europeans. But at least she was providing a service, and in the mean-time she made her plans to build a fine new Cecil, just as quickly as the availability of building supplies and the necessary approval of the Administration permitted.

Mrs Stewart made a lot of money — there was nowhere else in Lae for the traveller to stay — and her success was not lost on Joe Bourke, who all his life was a shrewd and successful businessman. And he knew that other hoteliers were starting up in other towns. In Rabaul, the only public accommodation was provided by the Civilian Hostel operated by the Production Control Board and managed by Mrs Valentine. In May, 1947, the Board decided to get out of the accommodation business, and the Hostel was sold by tender to a group of local businessmen, among whom was A.J. Gaskin,

Kokopo Hotel, Kokopo in 1916, near Rabaul, built by the Germans when Kokopo was the centre of administration for German New Guinea.

Rabaul Hotel, 1916.

who before the war had owned the Cosmopolitan Hotel. The Civilian Hostel now became the new Cosmopolitan. Mrs Dorothy Stewart (no kin to Flo) was brought up from Melbourne as the manageress.

Rabaul, capital of the Mandated Territory before the war, had once supported many hotels. A number were small, cheap Chinese establishments — the Chin Hing ('Cheerful, Bright, Comfortable') and the Chee Jour Gnee ('The Home of Travellers and Tourists') were probably the best known. The latter was owned and managed by the famous Ah Chee, lauded on his death in December, 1933, as 'the most popular Chinaman in the Territory'. The principal hotel was the Rabaul, managed for years by the well-known E. (Tex) Roberts. Another leading establishment was the Pacific. Seven miles out of town was the North Coast Hotel. The Toma Hotel advertised itself as the 'Health Resort of the Pacific'. There was a pleasant pub at Kokopo, run by the popular Mrs Gilmore.

Joe Bourke decided to enter the hotel trade, and Wau seemed to him a logical place. The town was growing, and at nearby Bulolo, BGD Ltd. was rapidly rebuilding the town and re-commissioning the giant gold dredges. He succeeded in obtaining a fine site in the centre of town, and in mid-1948, the Wau Hotel (the name 'Kaindi' was abandoned) opened for business.

2

Birth of a Brewing Company

Territorians have always been mighty drinkers. The heat and humidity of the tropics, combined with the easy lifestyle that was one of the most attractive features of life in the PNG of colonial times, produced conditions conducive to steady drinking.

The first Territorians to return after the war found the alcohol position grim. Post-war importations by sea commenced with the arrival of the S.S. *Marella* in Port Moresby on 29 November, 1945, but she carried only essential foodstuffs and building materials. To ease the local situation, the Army Canteen Service released some stocks of liquor, together with foods, general merchandise, hardware and tobacco, but this was merely a temporary measure.

Beer was always the favourite drink of the Territorian. Before the war, the big Australian breweries held the lion's share of the market, although the products of famous world breweries were also freely available. Hard

Papua Hotel ('the top pub'), Port Moresby, as it was in the early 1930s.

11

liquor, too, was consumed in great quantity, particularly rum, whisky and gin.

No beer was manufactured in PNG. It was all imported. Some draught beer was available, but only in the larger centres. It first went on sale at the Papua Hotel in Port Moresby, in 1928. Visiting ships — particularly those of BP & Co. and the German and Dutch packet companies — served draught beer in their bars, and the arrival of one of these vessels in the more isolated ports of PNG attracted local drinkers as a magnet.

Like virtually all consumer products in Australia immediately following the war, beer was in short supply. It was strictly rationed, and beer 'droughts' were common. The big brewing companies found that they could sell all they could manufacture, and more, in Australia. Traditional markets like PNG were all but ignored, although such leading brands as Victoria Bitter, Fosters Lager and KB Lager were regularly advertised in the pages of *Pacific Islands Monthly*, and later in the first post-war newspaper, the *South Pacific Post*, which began to appear in September, 1950. The major Australian breweries supplied the big PNG companies — principally, Burns Philp & Co., W.R. Carpenter & Co., and Steamships Trading Co. — with small consignments of their product on a quota basis, based on the value of pre-war orders. The quantity supplied was quite inadequate to meet the demand. The result was that Australian beer in PNG in the early post-war years was a very scarce, and expensive, commodity. Of the total of 397,000 gallons of beer imported in 1949-50, only 41,000 gallons came from Australia. Black-market prices were often demanded. Men paid up to eight shillings and six pence for a single precious bottle, and consumed it in secret.

The bulk of the beer imported came from overseas, from the ends of the earth. The number of brands in circulation was extraordinary; the taste of some lingers unpleasantly in the memories of old Territorians to the present day. Perhaps the most evil of these products was Revolver Brand, a black and bitter brew tasting strongly of liquorice manufactured in Scotland, for the African trade, it was rumoured. On most people, it acted as a strong aperient. Adorned with a white label on which was emblazoned a black hand clutching a large pistol, Revolver Brand was imported by Mark Schultz, an old Goldfield identity who in July, 1948, was granted a liquor licence for the first new rural hotel to be built in PNG after the war, at Mumeng, half-way between Lae and Wau.

One of the first palatable beers to be available in reasonable quantity was Pabst Blue Ribbon, in cans, from America. Barclay's Lager was sold in cartons of two dozen tin cans that strongly resembled a well-known silver polish, and of course it was invariably called 'Brasso'. It sold for thirty shillings per carton, and there were those who held that it was well nick-named. Among the many scores of brands available at different times were Waitamata and Halloran's Pale Ale from New Zealand. England contributed Tennant's Pale Ale and Allsop's Lager (the latter was unkindly known as 'Allslopp's'). Through the East, via Hong Kong, came such brands as Elephant, San Miguel, Three Horses, Red Horse. Some good brews came from famous European brewers: Beck's, sold in massive wooden cases of 48 x 28-ounce bottles, the necks heavily wrapped in foil; Tuborg — a favourite in PNG for many years; St. Pauli Girl; Carlsberg. There was even a Chinese brand, which was for a time the only beer available in Madang, where it sold for two pounds per dozen twenty-ounce bottles. It was terrible beer, but as the saying went, 'Territorians would drink anything through an oily rag'.

Varying wildly in quality as they did, these beers had two things in common; they were expensive, and their availability was unpredictable. All too often a drinker would become accustomed to the taste of a particular product, and then find that it was off the market.

Joe Bourke started to toy with the idea of establishing a brewery in PNG. 'I could see no sense in transporting beer in bulky bottles over thousands of miles from Europe, Asia and Australia, when New Guinea contained an abundance of the principal component — water,' he wrote. He kept his ideas to himself, but when a batch of 3,000 stainless steel barrels were advertised for tender in a war disposals sale at Lae, he purchased them cheaply. They were each of seven and a half gallon capacity, and looked to Joe to be ideal beer containers.

Joe Bourke was astute enough to realize that the European population of PNG was going to increase rapidly. Australia had accepted a United Nations Trusteeship over the old Mandated Territory and was committed to the political and economic development of PNG. In a few years, a rich market for soundly made local beer would surely exist. Hotels — including his own — were already finding it difficult to obtain sufficient imported beer to satisfy their customers. Australian breweries did not seem overanxious to fill the gap, but Joe Bourke decided to give them a go.

In 1949 Bourke took one of his stainless steel containers and set off for Australia to see whether or not he could arrange for regular supplies of draught beer for the Wau Hotel. He took his barrel to Tooth & Co., the big Sydney brewers, where he had a long talk with the General Manager, Thomas Watson. Joe was chagrined to find that his barrels could not be used as containers for draught beer without expensive modifications, and in any case, the beer was just not available. As much as Tooth & Co. would like to assist, the fact remained that beer rationing was in force in New South Wales. Sydney hotels were selling draught beer for only three hours per day, five days per week, and for four hours on Saturdays. Bottled beer, too, was scarce and was sold only to regular customers. None of the precious fluid could be spared for the Wau Hotel.

Rather deflated by this interview, and wondering gloomily what he was going to do with 3,000 barrels, Joe Bourke went off to Hyde Park to think things over. He sat on a bench, cuddling his barrel, watching the girls pass by and soaking up the sun. Then he spied an old friend, Tom Yeomans, similarly engaged on another park bench. Yeomans was now living in Sydney, and the two friends promptly fell into a conversation about the good old days. Inevitably, their talk soon turned to the subject of beer. Joe mentioned his half-formed dream of setting up a brewery in PNG, and soon the two men were deep in a discussion of the pros and cons, and then of ways and means.

The biggest hurdle was, obviously, finance. Neither Bourke nor Yeomans had any idea of the cost of establishing a brewery from scratch, but whatever the amount, it would be beyond their combined resources. Obviously a company would have to be formed, but initial funds would be required to get the project off the ground. Both felt confident that there would be support for a brewery in PNG. They decided to press on.

Joe Bourke was booked to return to New Guinea the following day on the 'Bird of Paradise' service operated by Qantas Empire Airways. (The company proudly advertised that the flying time, Sydney to Port Moresby, in 'fast, modern DC3 airliners', was just under thirteen hours!) 'Tom agreed to organise the Sydney end — capital, equipment and staff,' Bourke wrote in an account of the early days of the enterprise. 'My job was to organise the New Guinea end — some more capital, water analysis. statistics of beer imports, land, and a licence to brew.'

Early in 1950, a Brewery Syndicate was formed at Wau, and sufficient capital was subscribed to allow the Syndicate to acquire land. It was intended that the Brewery be established somewhere in the Wau Valley. Joe Bourke then turned to the problem of securing a licence to brew beer. At that time the liquor legislation in force in both Papua and the Trust Territory of New Guinea contained no provision for the issue of brewing licences. The Administrator of PNG, Colonel J.K.Murray, was not at first in favour of a brewery, but eventually official opposition was overcome and steps were taken to amend the liquor ordinances.

A Qantas DC3 'Bird of Paradise' landing at Wewak.

Joe Bourke had worked very hard, but at this stage the proposed brewery was little more than an exercise on paper, backed by promises of financial support but little actual cash. The proposal could well have fizzled out, but for a decision by Percival Alfred Yeomans to risk a substantial investment.

Perce Yeomans, a successful company director with business premises in Elizabeth Street, Sydney, was Tom Yeomans's nephew. When his uncle first raised the question of investing in a brewery in New Guinea, Perce Yeomans was not impressed. In a recent interview with the author, Yeomans recalled his discussions with Tom with a good deal of amusement.

'You know, I've never listened to such a half-baked proposal,' he said. 'As a business proposition, it was hopeless. All Tom and Joe really had was an idea. They hadn't done much spadework. They didn't know anything about breweries, how they are built, how they're operated, how much they cost. If anyone else but Tom had approached me, I'd have had nothing to do with it. I thought to myself, "You're both mad". Still, I knew an expert on breweries, slightly. Fred Howard. His wife and mine had met overseas on holidays, and later I gave his sons work on my farm. I said to Tom, "Look, I'll talk this over with Fred Howard". Howard agreed to fly up to New Guinea and have a look.'

John Frederick Howard was a brewery construction engineer, the Australian representative of A.Ziemann Breweries of Ludwigsburg, near Stuttgart, Germany. He flew to Port Moresby, where he was met by Joe Bourke. The idea of locating the brewery at Wau had by this time been abandoned by the Syndicate, principally because of the high cost of transport to and from this inland centre.

'I was able to give Howard accurate beer import figures and the results of water analyses', Bourke later wrote. 'I showed him three different brewery sites in Port Moresby, which he condemned out of hand. Burns

Philp had constructed a prefabricated steel shed in Scratchley Road, Badili, in which they had installed a lot of ex-Army laundry equipment. During our search for a suitable location we inspected this one, and Howard decided on the spot that it was the only place suitable for our purpose. He said we would require at least one acre of freehold land, an easement over a cement water tank close by, and a six-feet easement to convey brewery effluent to the sea. Unless these arrangements could be made, there would be no brewery in New Guinea. He left by air for Australia next morning'.

On his return from Port Moresby, Howard reported to Perce Yeomans. 'Put in 500 quid, no more,' he recommended. Then, as an afterthought, he added, 'You know, it could just prove to be a real goer, if you feel like taking a bit of a gamble'. That was enough for Perce Yeomans. He decided to underwrite the project. Surely, he thought, the big merchant companies in PNG — Carpenters, Steamships, Burns Philp — would take shares in such a promising enterprise.

In this hope he was to be disappointed. The only big initial investor, apart from Joe Bourke and the two Yeomans, was another old Morobe Goldfield hand, mining engineer Thomas Zoffman.

Meanwhile, Joe Bourke was faced with the problem of acquiring the Badili site from Burns Philp. BP, the Big Firm, was notoriously hard to deal with (old Territorians held that the initials of the company stood for 'Bloody Pirates') and had always been reluctant to part with land. Moreover, the General Manager of Burns Philp (New Guinea) Limited was E.J. Frame. 'I had known Eddie Frame for years,' Joe recalled. 'Tough as they come, a great poker player, and no holds barred in business. I knew the going was not to be easy.'

Circumstances combined to provide Joe Bourke with a solution. Burns Philp was not really interested in operating a laundry, and did so only because no alternative service was available. Through its subsidiary, Port Moresby Freezing Co., Burns Philp ran two hotels, the Moresby and the Papua, and laundry services were also required for the BP ships on the PNG run. Their laundry equipment at Badili was worn out, and overdue for replacement. The company decided to sell off the equipment and lease the site and premises, letting somebody else spend the hard cash required to install modern laundry facilities.

It was common knowledge that two local businessmen were engaged in negotiations with BP for a lease of the Badili laundry. 'I approached one of them', Joe Bourke wrote, 'and offered him £2,000 commission if he could purchase, not lease, on my behalf the freehold and easements we required, the top price to be no more than £10,000 cash. After three days of secret meetings and nerve wracking negotiations, the deal was finally concluded. When the documents were signed, sealed and delivered, I called on Eddie Frame and told him of our plan to build a brewery on the Badili site. I'll never forget his reactions. He considered he'd been hoodwinked, and he swore that as far as BP & Co. were concerned, there'd be no beer brewed in

16

New Guinea!'.

Freehold title over the Badili land was now held jointly by Brewery Syndicate members: Joe Bourke; Tom Yeomans; Norman Hansen White, mining engineer and planter; Norman Roberts Wilde, miner; Austin Peter Ireland, miner; Alice Bowring, miner; Marjorie June White, wife of solicitor Norman White. All were residents of Wau.

While these negotiations were in train, Fred Howard — retained as consultant by Perce Yeomans and Joe Bourke on behalf of the Syndicate — went to Europe to purchase machinery and equipment. The necessary funds were provided by Perce Yeomans, with contributions from Tom Yeomans and Tom Zoffman. For an outlay of almost £18,000 Sterling, Howard acquired a small brewhouse from the A.Ziemann concern, Ludwigsburg; a semi-automatic rotary bottle filler from a firm in Mannheim; and from B.Ashworth and Co., London, a malt mill, storage tanks, bottle cleaning machinery, a pasteuriser, wort cooler, and wort clarifier. This was only the beginning. A modern brewery is a complex installation. A great deal more cash was to be laid out before the first beer was brewed, but certainly the essentials had been obtained.

On 9 October, 1950, a meeting of the Brewery Syndicate was held at Wau. It was agreed that a company be formed, to be called 'South Pacific Brewery Limited' and located at Port Moresby. Capital was set at £150,000. Fred Howard was appointed a Syndicate member free of all calls up to the time of the formation of the company. It was agreed that the Badili freehold land, easements and buildings would be sold by the Syndicate to the company for the sum of £15,000. Howard would be responsible for the installation of the brewery at Badili, and would find a brewer and the necessary technical staff.

Fred Howard quickly found his brewer. In 1949, Mr and Mrs Rudolf Meier emigrated from Switzerland to Australia. Meier, a Hungarian, was a highly-trained master brewer, who had learned his art in Germany. As a young man, he had assisted his uncle to establish a brewery for Malayan Breweries Ltd. in Singapore, producing the famous Tiger brand beer. When the Second World War broke out, Meier was Brewmaster at a brewery in Alexandria, Egypt. He was an enemy alien and by rights should have been interned for the duration, but wars are fought on beer and Meier was allowed to continue his work, under supervision.

Meier did not find life in post-war Australia very pleasant. He spoke poor English, and although he possessed a quick but seldom-revealed sense of humour, he was plainly a foreigner and as such, resented by some Australians. Quite by chance, Fred Howard was introduced to Rudi Meier at a cocktail party in Sydney, and soon afterwards Meier accepted the position of Brewmaster at the South Pacific Brewery.

'He is a fussy, educated man', wrote Tom Yeomans to Joe Bourke, 'and will need careful handling to keep contented. So on his first trip up there it would be wise for him not to meet too many people. He should meet

Norman White, Jimmy James etc, but not the general run of chaps, for he hates bad language...'.

Poor Meier! He was to encounter a lot of bad language in PNG, but he quickly demonstrated his ability as a brewer, and as a draftsman and builder. The planning, layout and construction of the brewery was to be largely his work.

On 25 January, 1951, a Certificate of Incorporation under the *Companies Ordinance* 1912-1926 of the Territory of Papua was issued in the name of South Pacific Brewery Limited by the acting Registrar of Companies, Colin Darbyshire. On the following day, the first meeting of the Board of Directors was held, at the office of Norman White, solicitor, Port Moresby, who had been handling the legal affairs of the Brewery Syndicate from the outset. Present at the meeting were P.A. and T. Yeomans and Joe Bourke, directors. Norman White and E.A. (Jimmy) James, public accountant, were present by invitation.

Perce Yeomans was appointed Chairman of the Board. James became Secretary of the company, and his office was the registered office of South Pacific Brewery Limited. An account was opened with the Port Moresby branch of the Bank of New South Wales, and the firm of Parish, Patience and McIntyre were appointed company solicitors. This old-established firm of Sydney solicitors had opened an office in Port Moresby in January, 1946, under the supervision of D.L.McIntyre, and had prepared the Memorandum and Articles of Association of the new company. These stated that the capital of the company was £150,000, divided into 50,000 preference shares of one pound each, and 100,000 ordinary shares, also of one pound.

Rapidly, the meeting ratified the purchase of the Badili property from the old Brewery Syndicate, and adopted the service agreement with Fred Howard. Applications for shares from the promoters of the company were produced; 13,500 ordinary shares were allocated to Perce Yeomans, and 6,250 each to Tom Yeomans and Tom Zoffman. They were also reimbursed for the money outlayed for equipment purchases.

A prospectus was approved, and it was resolved that applications for shares would be received from 2 February to 24 February, 1951.

Finally, Norman White tabled a brewer's licence issued under the authority of the newly amended *Liquor Ordinance* 1911-1950 of the Territory of Papua, dated 23 December, 1950.

South Pacific Brewery Limited was in business.

3

`It's Bloody Good Beer!´

The company was in existence, but the production of beer was a long way off. The time had now come for supporters of this enterprise, born and nurtured on the Morobe Goldfield, to put up their cash. There was no lack of applicants for the shares, but certain persons who had earlier expressed enthusiasm failed to apply. Nevertheless, when 50,000 ordinary shares were allocated by resolution of the directors on 20 April, 1951, the list of shareholders contained the names of many of the best known citizens of Wau and Bulolo, and other Territory centres. There were businessmen among them, and housewives, prospectors, tradesmen, public servants, seamen, engineers.

The principal shareholder was Perce Yeomans, who took more shares to build his total holding to 15,500. Tom Zoffman held 6,750, Tom Yeomans 6,250, and Joe Bourke 3,000. Norman Wilde held 4,000 and Alice Bowring 1,800. Other investors held parcels ranging from fifty to 1,000 shares. Among them were H.J.McKenzie, Mrs John Hohnen, Mrs Lars Bergstrand, Mrs Norman Hansen White, Mrs L.E.Ashton, R.F.Bunting, H.P.Seale, Miss K.E.Vellacott-Jones, J.K.McCarthy, Mr and Mrs Norman White, K.M.Llewellyn, W.C. De Rusett, W.J.McPherson, W.B.Blackley, and many others.

Norman Wilde was an authentic war hero. The brother of Mrs Doris Booth of *Cliffside* (herself renowned as the 'Angel of Edie Creek', for her work in controlling an epidemic of dysentery in 1926), he spent many years mining on the Morobe field before the Pacific war. Wilde held a private flying licence and when the Japanese invaded New Guinea in 1942, he joined with commercial pilot Eric Stephens to snatch 180 civilians from their path and evacuate them to safety in a series of dangerous flights in the ancient Avro monoplane, *Faith in Australia*, once owned by C.E.T.Ulm, Sir Charles Kingsford-Smith's co-pilot on the epic trans-Pacific flight of 1928. In a well-nigh incredible exploit, Wilde found an abandoned DH Moth biplane at Port Moresby, commandeered it, and flew eleven Chinese from Salamaua to safety. The Moth had an official carrying capacity of one passenger.

Alice Bowring, too, was a well-loved Goldfield identity. 'Mum' Bowring — as she was universally known — was a plump, grey-haired widow but a miner still, and full of the joy of living, always ready for a drink, a yarn or a good deed. In the early 1930s she had kept a boarding house at Edie Creek, but at heart she was always a goldminer.

H.J.McKenzie was Mining Registrar of the Morobe Goldfield, and a future amateur golf champion of PNG. John Hohnen was managing director of New Guinea Goldfields Ltd., and Lars Bergstrand ran Bulolo Gold Dredging Ltd. The Whites were old Wau residents; Norman Hansen came to New Guinea in the 1920s and mined gold on the Sepik as well as in the Morobe District. After the war he became a vegetable farmer at Wau. Norman, his son, was a barrister and solicitor, in practice in Port Moresby from 1946.

L.E.Ashton had a distinguished career as a field officer in the Papuan service. He served from 1916 to 1927, and then resigned to look for gold in the Sepik, the Highlands and on the Morobe field. During the war he was in the NGVR, the Coastwatchers and later in the Pacific Islands Regiment. He married Margaret, sister of R.F.Bunting. Bob Bunting mined gold at Edie Creek at the very beginning before taking over his late father's merchant firm, A.H.Bunting Ltd., based at Samarai. Bunting later became a nominated member of the PNG Legislative Council, from 1954 to 1961. As a soldier with the 8th Division during the war, Bunting became a POW when the Japanese captured Singapore. His was a very bad war.

H.P.Seale, at the time he became a shareholder in South Pacific Brewery Ltd., was Assistant District Officer, Wau Sub-District. Before the war, Bill Seale had been a Customs and Treasury officer, and was in charge of the Bulolo Post Office when war broke out. He served in ANGAU and the AIF, and went on to become a District Commissioner and an official member of the House of Assembly. J.K.McCarthy was District Commissioner of the New Britain District when he purchased his brewery shares. One of the most colourful figures in the PNG Public Service, Keith McCarthy began his career as a patrol officer in 1927, and finished as Director of Native Affairs in 1967. The intervening years found him exploring new country in the interior, serving as a Coastwatcher and with ANGAU during the war, and in later years an official member of the House of Assembly. Painter, writer and cartoonist, McCarthy was known throughout PNG. Kathleen Vellacott-Jones was the Administration's public relations officer; W.J.McPherson was superintendent of Postal Services; K.M.Llewellyn was a geologist with the Australasian Petroleum Company, leader of notable survey expeditions in the wilds of the Western Division. De Russet and Blackley were old Goldfield residents, one an electrical engineer and the other Secretary of Gold and Power Ltd., a mining company operating on the Upper Watut.

Support for South Pacific Brewery Ltd., then, was drawn from a wide variety of occupations. On 22 August, 1951, the directors resolved to raise an additional £50,000 by issuing further ordinary shares to existing shareholders, and the general public. Many other noted Territorians invested. Construction of the brewery was proceeding, and expenses were multiplying.

Rudolf Meier, who was now General Manager as well as Brewmaster, was a hard and consistent worker, and under his energetic direction the brewery complex rapidly assumed shape, despite frustrating shortages of building materials. His principal assistants were Fred Howard's son, Charles, and Jack Fitz, a Ziemann Breweries representative. Much of the work was subcontracted to identities like Wally Connelly and 'Lofty' Wolstenholme, electricians; A.E.Eldridge, plumber; and building contractor Jack Wilson. Wilson, a hard case, became notorious in PNG in 1957, when he was sent to gaol for eighteen months for unlawful possession of gold, together with Eric Woo and old Goldfields hand, Carlo Cavalieri, both of whom received sentences of twelve months.

By early October, 1951, Meier was able to report to a meeting of the directors that a residence at the Brewery was almost complete, excavations for the refrigeration buildings were well in hand, the settling tank was finished, and the engine room and bottling cellar within two weeks of completion. Some vital equipment was still in Germany, awaiting shipment.

Present at this meeting, as legal representative of the Bank of New South Wales — which had granted the company a working overdraft — was James Irwin Cromie, who thus began an active association with South Pacific Brewery that was to last until 1980.

Jim Cromie and his wife, Delphine, came to the Mandated Territory of New Guinea from Melbourne, in 1935. A solicitor, newly qualified, Cromie's first place of business was on the verandah of the old Wau Hotel. His cash resources were at first too low to allow him the luxury of a formal office. His fortunes soon changed. The biggest concern in the Wau Valley in 1935 was the mining company, New Guinea Goldfields Ltd. Retained by NGG, Jim Cromie was provided with a home and an office. In mid-1937 he moved to Rabaul where in 1940 he joined the NGVR. After the Japanese bombed Rabaul on 4 January, 1942, Cromie returned to Wau where he became Adjutant to the NGVR on the mainland. When the NGVR was absorbed into ANGAU, Jim Cromie became its chief legal officer. He was discharged at the end of 1945 and in February, 1946, returned to PNG, where he re-established his practice at Port Moresby. He was appointed solicitor to South Pacific Brewery Ltd. in August, 1952, replacing Norman White who had earlier replaced Parish, Patience and McIntyre.

Shipping problems were finally overcome, and Meier predicted to the first annual general meeting of South Pacific Brewery Ltd., on 21 April, 1952, that beer should be produced in August. Among those present at this meeting, as a delegate director for Joe Bourke, was Stephenson (Peter) Fox, an English-born, Australian-educated chartered accountant, poet, singer, political activist and public figure, who in 1982 was still living in PNG, at Goroka.

Production of beer depended upon the arrival of the brewhouse, which had been shipped from Germany to Sydney. It was due to arrive in Port Moresby on the MV *Bulolo*, on 21 June, 1952, and was to be installed by a German expert and an assistant from Australia.

The early availability of locally brewed beer was awaited with keen interest by Territory drinkers, and by hotel keepers and club managers. In most major Territory centres, licenced premises were under construction, and some from pre-war days were being resurrected. All would require beer.

By far the oldest hotels in PNG were the Papua and the Moresby, the Burns Philp hotels, known from the earliest times as the 'Top Pub' and the 'Bottom Pub'. The Port Moresby Hotel, as the Bottom Pub was originally titled, was built in 1910 by Tom McCrann. A sprawling, two-storied structure, McCrann proudly advertised it in the *Papuan Times* as 'The Premier Hotel in Papua', with plunge and shower baths and the most modern appointments and conveniences. A 'first class white cook' was employed, and 'a supply of fresh vegetables and fruit contracted for to arrive by every steamer'. The Billiard Room was equipped 'with one of Alcock's finest tables in the hands of an expert'. The premises were 'brilliantly lighted with Acetylene Gas'.

In fact the Port Moresby Hotel was a badly ventilated, hot, uncomfortable establishment, providing barely tolerable board and lodging for thirty-two shillings per week. The rival hotel, the Papua, was only marginally better. Construction of this hotel began in 1909, just before the discovery of the Lakekamu Goldfield, but the builder's finance ran out before it could be completed. In 1910 the shell was purchased by Tim Ryan, who fitted it out

Papua Hotel and Tim Ryan's transport fleet, c1912.

and opened it in early 1911 as the Papua Hotel. Not to be outdone by his rival, Tim Ryan also advertised his hotel as being 'brilliantly lighted with Acetylene Gas'. The hotel, he promised, would be 'run on first class lines. An excellent cuisine, clean and airy bedrooms, cool balconies. Good stabling. Only the Best of Wines and Spirits Stocked'. Ryan provided full board and lodging for seven pounds per month. Despite his glowing words, Ryan's pub, too, left a great deal to be desired.

In 1974 the author interviewed ex-Resident Magistrate A.E.Cridland at Tufi, where the old man had lived since his retirement from the Papuan Service. Cridland came to Port Moresby as a youngster in July, 1913, and he stayed for a time at Ryan's Papua Hotel.

'It was built in typical North Queensland style,' he recalled. 'Corrugated iron, with the lounge, bar, billiard and dining rooms downstairs, and upstairs a long verandah, with little poky bedrooms each with an iron cot, a mosquito net and a small dressing-table — nothing much else.

'At the time I arrived there was a party of miners in from the Lakekamu, on their annual trip to Port for a spree and a refit. There were about twenty of them. They were typical miners of that day — rough men, who had followed gold all over the world. One had been on the Klondike. They made things pretty lively, I can tell you!

'First thing they did was go to Baldwin's store[1] and buy new suits of pyjamas, with long sleeves and trousers. These were their dress suits while in Port. Nothing on their feet, no socks or shoes. They spent their days in the little annexe to the bar, where there was an old piano. The hotel gardener, Syd Bradfield, could play a bit, and that's all they wanted. They'd sing and drink beer, all day and all night. Beck's Lager was their favourite. It was brought out from Germany on the Norddeutscher Lloyd ships, en route to Rabaul. Now and again one of them would pour a bottle of Beck's down the back of the piano, just to oil the works. They'd sing old shanties and drink — they had an astounding capacity, after a year out in the bush. They never stopped! At night time you'd go up to your room to sleep, and find a drunken miner had got there first! It didn't matter, though, you'd just wander along the verandah and turn in on the first empty bed you came across. Oh, it was some pub!'

In 1928, both hotels were purchased by the Burns Philp subsidiary, Port Moresby Freezing Company. Mrs E.McGrath, who had previously operated the Matunga and Morinda Boarding Houses, was installed as manageress of the Papua. A new lounge and dining room were added, but the tone of the Papua was hardly genteel. Mrs McGrath, an ex-stewardess of the BP vessel, *Matunga*, was celebrated for her rough and ever-ready tongue. Around 1933 the Papua Hotel and the Moresby were merged and in 1937 Burns Philp decided to rebuild them both. The new Moresby Hotel, built alongside the old, opened on 23 February, 1939. The Papua, intended

1 C.R.Baldwin was a general merchant and shipowner, agent for the Royal Dutch Packet Co., who had a store on the site of the present BNG building.

Hotel Cecil, Lae.

to be the 'first luxury hotel in New Guinea', was completed at great expense in November, 1941, just in time to be taken over by the Army during the Pacific war. The Moresby suffered the same fate.

When the fighting ceased, only the Moresby was opened to the public for the Papua had been so badly knocked about by the armed forces during the war that it had to be completely renovated. A contract for the work was let to John Stubbs and Sons in September, 1946. Completed at a cost that would 'stagger guests', in the words of E.J.Frame at the cocktail party that marked the official opening on 26 September, 1947, the Papua provided pleasant accommodation for forty-four guests, and could seat 120 in the dining room. The whole history of the new Papua, said Eddie Frame, paraphrasing the famous words of Churchill during the Battle of Britain, could be summed up thus: 'Never has so little been accomplished in so long, and for so much'.

In Lae, the foundations of Flora Stewart's new Hotel Cecil were laid in February, 1950. Constructed on the Voco Point site of the pre-war Cecil, the new hotel was opened on 27 June, 1952. Although Mrs Stewart had spent more than £100,000 on the Cecil, it was still far from being completed. A huge, two-storied affair of uncertain design, it could seat 200 guests in the dining room. Two underground water tanks held 57,000 gallons of rainwater. The fifty-one bedrooms were complete with 'every modern convenience', the *South Pacific Post* optimistically reported. The big Bamboo Bar of the Cecil attracted the town's drinkers in droves, and the sales of beer were enormous. 'It is now six years since Mrs Stewart first decided to build a grand new hotel', reported the newspaper, 'and she is as proud, at the moment, as a child with a new toy'. She had, indeed, battled official indifference and material shortages of every kind to achieve her dream. This did not surprise old friends of the indomitable Flo Stewart.

In 1951, old hands Jack and Florence Gilmore began the construction of the Madang Hotel, completed in April, 1952. It was then billed as 'the most modern in the Territory', with accommodation for twenty-eight

24

guests. The first manager was Reg Vogler, and bed and breakfast was available for twenty-five shillings. At about the same time, Mrs Ellen Pitt was opening a small guest house at Goroka, which later evolved into the Goroka Hotel. The widow of old Territorian Mark Pitt, Ellen was a kindly hostess, providing 'just about the perfect home from home', in the words of a correspondent in the *South Pacific Post*.

The Papua New Guinea of colonial times was a great place for clubs. Much of the liquor consumed in the Territory was supplied by the clubs, of which there were a great variety. As with the hotels, the clubs of PNG were destroyed during the war, or went out of active existence, and the early post-war years saw the birth of many new ones, as well as the resurrection of a number of the old.

One of the first new clubs was the Lae Social and Sports Club, formed in August, 1946. In October of that year, the New Britain Club opened its doors. It was modelled along the lines of the gracious old Rabaul Club, now defunct. The entry fee was five pounds, and the annual subscription a like sum. The Club committee initially found it very difficult to obtain beer supplies. Local merchants could not assist and the club began to import its own.

Unhappily, the extraordinary post-war demand for accommodation in the capital resulted in a steady deterioration of the services provided by both hotels, as more and more guests were jammed into space designed for the comfort of a select few. Their bar trade was heavy, and constant. The basement under the old Moresby Hotel building became the 'Snake Pit' bar, of dubious memory. In March, 1955, the crew of a Qantas Skymaster complained to a *South Pacific Post* reporter of the 'sullen and arrogant' servants at the Papua hotel, calling it 'one of the worst they had ever stayed at'. The food was 'terrible' and the whole establishment 'took the cake'. Other guests questioned by the reporter whole-heartedly agreed. The hotel had slipped badly.

Port Moresby folk were able to obtain accommodation and alcoholic refreshment at another hostelry from March, 1951. In this month a hotel licence was granted to Mrs Dorothea Woodlands — later Troeth — for premises at Rouna, some thirty minutes drive up the Astrolabe Range, along a rough road. In 1923, Mrs E.King had built the Migagi Chalet on the site, and during the war a convalescent centre was located nearby, by the Red Cross. Both establishments were eventually taken over by the Army.

Mrs Woodlands came to Port Moresby in 1948, as caterer for the new Papua Hotel. She took over the Department of Civil Aviation Mess in 1949, and in 1950 purchased Mrs King's old property at Rouna. It was badly run down, but she converted it into a rambling, unpretentious hotel of considerable charm. 'Woody's Pub' became famous, a 'must' for overseas visitors to PNG. She built up a private zoo, which at one time contained wallabies, possums, pythons, crocodiles, tree-climbing kangaroos and many birds, including birds-of-paradise. Her celebrated hat collection began in the early 1950s, when a rugby league team from Mareeba, North Queensland, visited the pub. A team supporter, a very little man wearing a very big hat, caught Woody's eye. She offered to toss him for the hat against a dozen bottles of beer. He lost, and the hat went on the bar wall, the first of some 160, of infinite variety, that were to be displayed there over the following quarter-century.

Other new hotels were being established in the Trust Territory of New Guinea. In 1949, work began in Rabaul on a hotel for A.W.Brown, to be called the Ascot. Located in Mango Avenue, the Ascot opened for business in August, 1950.

In November, 1946, it was announced that the Kokopo Club was shortly to be revived. The Lae and Services Club opened in 1947. In January, 1948, plans were prepared for the rebuilding of the old New Guinea Club, at Rabaul. An RSL Club was born at Madang. The Madang Recreation Club received its liquor licence in July, 1948; liquor was in such short supply that members were advised that drinks would be available to members only 'on several afternoons and evenings each week'.

In December, 1949, the Committee of the Kavieng Club purchased the site of the pre-war Bank of New South Wales for a new residential club. The first concrete foundation post was laid on 27 January, 1950. There was an urgent need for residential accommodation at Kavieng. Meals were available for travellers at Tsang Tsang's Chinese Restaurant, but there was nowhere at all for them to stay.

Construction of a new RSL Club at Rabaul began in June, 1949, and the building was completed on Christmas Eve. In short order, the club had 300 members, and was voted 'a tremendous success'. Lae's new RSL Club was officially opened in May, 1952.

By 1953, licenced Aviat Clubs were in existence at Lae, Madang and Konedobu. A number of licenced sporting and social clubs were operating: Qantas Social Club and Golf Club, at Lae; the Sepik Club at Wewak; The Wau Club and Golf Club at Wau; the Bulolo Golf Club; the Manus Sports Club; the Goroka Sports Club; the Madang Golf Club; the Sogeri Country Club; the RSL Club, Samarai, and in Port Moresby the APC, Golf, RSL, Public Service, Paga, Papua, Aquatic, and Konedobu Clubs. Some of these had begun in the early post-war years. They sold a lot of beer.

It was not to be expected that liquor importers would look with equanimity on the prospect of losing a good slice of their market to a local brewery. In August, 1952, Rudolf Meier announced that South Pacific Brewery now expected to have its first beer on the market by the end of October. Both bottled and draught beer would be distributed in the company's own bottles purchased in Australia and in ten-gallon stainless steel kegs, also of Australian origin. 'The beer will be similar in taste to a well-known Sydney lager,' Meier told a *South Pacific Post* reporter. He was not able to predict the selling price — this would depend upon the amount of excise charged by the Administration. There was no PNG legislation covering excise on beer brewed in the Territory, but this question was expected to be settled during the October sittings of the Legislative Council. The price, however, would certainly be less than that prevailing for imported beers.

New South Wales and Victorian breweries, alive to the threat to their products, acted quickly to counter the imminent release of South Pacific beer. In August it was reported that quota supplies of Australian beer to the major Territory importers were to be increased immediately. 'The supplies are expected to fulfill most of the Territory's requirements,' said a spokesman. 'The management of one Moresby club hopes to sell Australian beer only when quotas are increased.' Both Burns Philp & Co. and Steamships Trading Co. confirmed that they would soon be receiving much greater supplies of Australian beer. 'People like the taste,' said the Port Moresby manager of BP, 'and will drink it in preference to imported beer.' The major thrust came from the Carlton and United Breweries and Tooth & Co. The big Sydney grocery firm, McIlrath's Pty. Ltd., announced that Swan Export Lager was now readily available for shipment to PNG residents, at twenty-six shillings and sixpence per dozen bottles in wooden cases containing forty-eight bottles.

Territory drinkers were cynical about this sudden rush of hitherto scarce Australian beer. In the year ended June, 1951, more than 2.5 million bottles of beer had been imported into PNG; less than 22 per cent of this had come from Australia. Obviously, it took the threat of competition to force a change.

The front page of the *South Pacific Post* for 7 November, 1952, featured a fetching headline: 'The Beer is Good. Hic! I Know'. The article that followed was written by a staff reporter, who had been invited by Rudi Meier to taste a pre-release sample of the first South Pacific brew. His comments gladdened the hearts of the brewery directors, and the Territory's beer drinkers —

'I can confidently say...it's good. A typical first-class Australian draught beer with a fine malty flavour and a thick, creamy head. The foam adhered to the side of the glass even when empty. It has more 'body' than any bottled beer I have tasted in Port Moresby...'.

The manager of Port Moresby Freezers, W.H.Johns, also tasted the brew and said that it was 'better than any bottled beer we are selling'. He advised that the 'latest cooling apparatus' would be arriving that day on the *Bulolo* for installation at the two PMF hotels.

Despite E.J.Frame's earlier opposition to South Pacific Brewery, and the promise of increased Australian beer supplies, he was a realist. His company operated two hotels through Port Moresby Freezers. Their customers would demand draught beer, which would have to be obtained from South Pacific. Local bottled beer, too, would be cheaper than the imported product. E.V.Crisp, managing director of Steamships — BP's major competitor in Port Moresby — was also anxious to sell local beer in his licenced outlets.

In October, the Legislative Council passed the new liquor bill, regulating the brewing and supply of beer in the Territory. Duty on locally brewed beer was set at three shillings and six pence per gallon, one shilling and six pence less than the rate on imported beer.

In November, agreement was reached between South Pacific Brewery, retailers — BP & Co., STC and others — and the Administration Prices Controller on the supply and retail selling price of local beer. The retail price of a dozen standard bottles was set at one pound thirteen shillings and ninepence, plus a returnable bottle deposit, considerably less than imported beers.

South Pacific draught and bottled beer went on public sale in Port Moresby on 26 November, 1952. Draught beer came on at the Moresby and Papua hotels at 10 am, selling for one shilling and one penny per seven ounce glass in the bars, and one shilling and fourpence in the lounges (which caused many grumbles). A survey of drinkers packing both hotels conducted by the *South Pacific Post* indicated that the majority found the beer very much to their taste, although there were some dissenters.

Barmaid Paula Stitt delivered an expert's opinion. 'It's very good. The taste is nearly as good as any Australian brew. I think the draught is better than the bottled'. Others ranged widely in their comments —

'Very nice, light taste. Seems to be more in it than you think'.

'Excellent. Smooth taste. I like it'.

'Really colossal. At the price, who'd complain?'

'I'll form an opinion when I wake up tomorrow'.

'The first taste wasn't too bad, but I've been drinking so many other beers for so long that the preservatives taste I'd acquired did not appreciate the beer until the eighth glass'.

'Best beer they've ever had up here. A very good taste with a powerful boot'.

'Miles ahead of any bottled beer'.

'It's drinkable, and better than Fosters'.

'Not too good in the present state. Should be given longer to mature'.

'Good draught beer, but a bit watery'.

Some drinkers complained of a slight aftertaste of onions, particularly from the bottled beer, but most agreed with the words of one stalwart —

'It's bloody good beer!'

4

Competition

South Pacific Brewery Limited in January, 1953, was a modest concern, with a brewing capacity of 150,000 gallons of beer per year, and employing a staff of seven Europeans and twenty-five Papua New Guineans, almost all of them from the Kerema Sub-District of what was then the Gulf District.

Very little South Pacific beer was initially available outside Post Moresby. A small trial shipment was sent to Rabaul in January, where it sold for four shillings and sixpence per bottle, a high price much resented by the drinkers of that town. The company promised that when the brewery was in a position to make larger shipments, the selling price would be much lower. Even before production commenced it was obvious that a greater output of beer from the brewery was required, and another £50,000 was raised by a share issue to finance expansions. On 27 November, 1952, at an Extraordinary General Meeting of the company, the authorised capital was increased to £500,000.

In Port Moresby, the company was in a strong position. The product was acceptable to most, and sold for less than the imports. The inevitable happened. 'Beer Price War Is On!', ran a headline in the *South Pacific Post* on 30 January. Steamships Trading Company were long-time distributors of one of the most popular of the imported beers, Beck's Lager. Although they also sold SP beer, STC intended to keep handling Beck's. Before SP came onto the market, STC sold Beck's at forty-eight shillings per dozen, retail. Now they dropped the price to thirty-seven shillings and ninepence, which included the bottle deposit. To meet this, the price of SP lager was temporarily reduced to twenty-seven shillings per dozen in ten-dozen lots, ex-brewery, plus a bottle deposit of four shillings per dozen.

By May, 1953, Beck's was down to twenty-nine shillings and sixpence per dozen, or five pounds fifteen shillings per case of forty-eight bottles. Then another merchant entered the fray. G.G. Smith & Co. were agents in Papua for another leading imported brand, Tuborg. After SP came on the market, the price of Tuborg dropped to thirty-five shillings per dozen, delivered free anywhere in the Port Moresby town area. By February, 1953, it was down to thirty-one shillings and sixpence with three shillings returned per dozen empty bottles. Tuborg went to twenty-seven shillings in June, and Smith's offered to pick up empties. In August, G.G. Smith & Co. were advertising this really fine, imported beer at the seemingly impossible price of twenty-one shillings per dozen! It was a great time for Tuborg drinkers. This price was maintained until the end of the year. Smith's could hardly have made money on these sales. (In April, 1954, G.G. Smith & Co. were taken over by Steamships.)

Throughout this trade war, the price of SP bottled lager was maintained at the original price; one pound thirteen shillings and ninepence per dozen, plus bottle deposit. Every gallon of SP made found a ready market. Territory drinkers were beginning to develop a taste for the local product, and some imported brands began to disappear. Towards the end of 1953 a new bottled SP beer, Export Lager, was introduced, selling for the slightly higher figure of one pound fifteen shillings and ninepence per dozen. In November, 1,750 dozen of the new product were shipped to Australia to test the market there, and Rudolf Meier announced that orders for another 5,000 dozen were still outstanding. Once Australian requirements were satisfied, a 'large order' for Export Lager from San Francisco would be shipped.

Slowly but surely, SP beer captured a modest share of the market. Victorian brands that had for many years been regarded as the standard by which all beers were judged — Fosters, Victoria Bitter, Melbourne Bitter — began to slip, although a big proportion of drinkers stayed with them. In August, 1953, 712 dozen bottles of Emu Bitter and Emu Lager, seized by Customs at Lae, were sold at auction for the extraordinary price of one shilling and ninepence per dozen. Burns Philp, distributors of Carlton and United beers, began to cut the price of Victorian bottled beer. Fosters was selling for forty-one shillings and sevenpence per dozen by the end of 1953, and six months later this beer, together with Victoria Bitter and Melbourne Bitter, was down to thirty-nine shillings and ninepence. THE DRUM column in the issue of *South Pacific Post* for 17 February, 1954, contained a significant little item —

'Times Change. The *Mangola* uploaded 2,000 dozen bottles of Australian beer from Lae last week for return to Australia. It couldn't be sold in Lae!'.

Few would have thought such a thing possible, before the introduction of South Pacific beer. Lae was now a strong market for SP, and early in 1954 agreement was reached with the Hotel Cecil, the RSL Club and the Lae Club for the installation of refrigerated beer dispensing units, to handle draught beer. Similar units were installed at the Port Moresby Golf Club, and the Aviat, Aquatic, Badili and Konedobu Clubs. Eventually, units of this type would be found in licenced premises all over Papua New Guinea, as SP beer increased in popularity.

At this time, too, an agreement was reached with the Royal Australian Navy at Manus for the sale of 75,000 gallons of beer. The Americans had built up an enormous base at Manus during the Pacific war, at enormous cost — $156 million, it was said. The then Australian Labour Government refused to allow the Americans to remain at the war's end, and in November, 1946, they pulled out of Manus. The superb Manus base was dismantled, and the magnificent equipment and installations deteriorated, were destroyed or were sold for a song. It soon became apparent, however, that world peace was not going to follow the war — Korea drove this lesson home — and the Australian Government took over the Manus base, partially restored it, and stationed considerable RAN and RAAF forces there. This was a grand potential market for SP beer. At a board meeting in November, 1953, the directors agreed to the purchase of 600 eighteen-gallon casks (kilderkins) for the purpose of supplying beer to the Navy, at an estimated cost of £15,000. Beer sales to the Navy were to be an important early source of income to South Pacific Brewery Ltd., particularly after Fred Howard was able to persuade the Burns Philp head office in Sydney to include Lombrum as a port of call for its vessels, thus overcoming the transport problem.

Business was so promising, in fact, that steps now had to be taken to further increase brewing capacity. In March, 1954, the Bank of New South Wales agreed to increase the South Pacific Brewery overdraft limit to £40,000, to finance the purchase of additional kilderkins (£10,000), extensions to the plant (£10,000) and to build a house for the assistant brewer. In April, the company announced that it expected to double its output within six months.

Hops used in the production of South Pacific beer were imported, at heavy cost. The price per ton was normally around £1,000 landed in Port Moresby, and in an effort to reduce this the company attempted to establish a hops industry in PNG, beginning in early 1954. With the assistance of the PNG administration and the NSW Department of Agriculture, experimental crops of hops were planted at Wau, Mount Hagen and Goroka, where the climate was considered ideal. However, the venture did not succeed. It was not possible to produce hops in the required quantities at an economic cost.

The first trading year of South Pacific Brewery Ltd. ended on 28 Februrary, 1954. It was a successful year, and the directors recommended the payment of a dividend for the first time, of 5 per cent. Of the amount of £7,656 available for distribution, all but £156 was returned to shareholders. (A 10 per cent dividend was paid the following year). In September, 1954, J.I.Cromie joined the board, which now included J.F.Howard, who was appointed managing director.

Although business was good, South Pacific Brewery Ltd. was by no means the major source of beer consumed in PNG at this time. In 1953/54, a total of 633,000 gallons of beer was imported: SP production was but 130,000 gallons, although work was well in hand on the extensions designed to double output.

In November, 1954, SP draught became available for the first time in bottles, and in the following April the brewery announced that a new lager, to be called 'Golden Lager', would soon be on the market. 'Under full production, we will be turning out 5,000 gallons of this new lager per month,' Rudolf Meier said. 'This will increase our total monthly production to about 20,000 gallons. Port Moresby consumers are taking about 60 per cent of our output. Most of the remainder is going to New Guinea, but we recently sent our first shipment to Fiji.' Meier also noted that the company would soon be producing carbon dioxide at the brewery, the surplus of which would be available for local soft drink manufacture.

The year 1955 was a momentous one for South Pacific Brewery. In December, a report appeared in the Sydney financial press-

'The controlling interest in South Pacific Brewery Limited has been sold to a Singapore company. The principal shareholders have sold 100,000 of South Pacific's 150,000 paid-up shares for £3 per share...'.

This was the first intimation that the general public in PNG had of the sale of the controlling interest in the local brewery. The Singapore company was Malayan Breweries Ltd., and the sale was negotiated by J.F.Howard with Max Lewis, general manager and director of Fraser and Neave and Malayan Breweries, and his technical director, Jack de Rijke. The price offered, £3 for each £1 share, was attractive enough to persuade Perce and Tom Yeomans, Tom Zoffman, Fred Howard himself, and others, to sell their shares. Joe Bourke was on leave at the time, and he retained his shares.

Malayan Breweries Ltd. (MBL) was formed in 1930, by soft-drink manufacturers Fraser and Neave Ltd. of Singapore and Heineken Technisch Beheer N.V. of Holland, the largest exporter of beers in the world. The technical expertise of Heineken combined with the marketing knowledge of Fraser and Neave guaranteed the success of the new venture. The first MBL brewery commenced producing Tiger Brand beer in 1931, and in 1941 the company acquired a second Singapore brewery. Tiger Brand beer was widely exported in Asia, before and after the Second World War.

The huge resources of the Heineken Group and MBL were now available to South Pacific Brewery Ltd. Both organisations were to maintain an active interest in the affairs of the Port Moresby brewery. In a brochure produced in 1975 by South Pacific Brewery, the relationship between the three companies was well summarised —

'Heineken of Holland provide the technical expertise for brewing and engineering, research and development, training and design, procurement of machinery and equipment, supervision of installations and production, and quality control. Malayan Breweries in turn provide commercial and marketing expertise'.

The mechanics of the transfer of control was handled by the creation of

a holding company, Pacific Holdings Ltd., at Goroka, wholly owned by MBL. Substantial numbers of shares were transferred to Pacific Holdings in February and May, 1956. With the transfer of control, Fred Howard ceased to be managing director of South Pacific Brewery Ltd. At the annual general meeting of the board on 25 May, 1956, the Yeomans and Fred Howard, no longer shareholders, did not offer themselves for re-election as directors. Howard was appointed commercial advisor to the company from 1 June at an annual fee of £1,000. The two Yeomans, co-pioneers of the company with Joe Bourke, now retired from the scene. Jim Cromie replaced Perce Yeomans as Chairman of the South Pacific board.

To fill the vacancies on the board, E.A.James and E.E.Kriewaldt were elected as directors. Ernest Emil Kriewaldt, a Victorian, came to Port Moresby in April, 1946, to work for the Administration. He resigned, and in September, 1950, opened a general store on a large site in Douglas Street. He sold a wide range of goods — including NSW and Victorian beer — and later pioneered self-service merchandising in the capital. He was the PNG agent for Peugeot cars, and sold a great number of them over the following ten years. Ernie Kriewaldt was an astute businessman, a welcome addition to the SP board.

E.A.James had been an outstanding figure in the commercial and political life of PNG for a quarter of a century. Secretary to South Pacific Brewery Ltd. since its birth, 'Jimmy' James brought an unrivalled knowledge of Papuan affairs to the deliberations of the board. Born in London in 1893, he came to Port Moresby in 1915 as a clerk with the Treasury Department, and in 1924 commenced practice as a public accountant. In 1925, as a sideline, he purchased the newspaper, *Papuan Courier*, which he edited until the Japanese invasion forced its closure. (It is interesting to note here that Jim Cromie was the first chairman of South Pacific Post Pty. Ltd., publishers of PNG's first post-war newspaper). James somehow found time in his busy life for public activity, and was moved by his admiration for the sons of Papua to act as local agent for Investors Limited, the Sydney-based company that financed the 1937 gold-seeking expedition led by Jack Hides and David Lyall to the Strickland headwaters, a tragic journey that ended in the death of Lyall, five carriers and of Hides himself, nine months after he returned. Jimmy James served as Deputy Controller for PNG of the Australian War Damage Commission from 1945 to 1947. He resumed his practice as a public accountant in Port Moresby in 1946, and was Chairman of the Port Moresby Town Advisory Council from its inception in 1952. He was elected as member of the Legislative Council for the Papuan Mainland in 1951 (a position he was to hold until his resignation in 1959, over the manner in which income tax was introduced to PNG). Nor did Jimmy James entirely foresake his old love, newspapers. For several years in the late 1950s, he was the author of a frequently controversial weekly column on public affairs, 'Have a Look', in the Friday issues of the *South Pacific Post* (the paper was then published twice weekly, on Tuesdays and Fridays).

James's comments were hard-hitting; he once branded the Minister for Territories, Paul Hasluck, 'dishonest' in his column, and called for his sacking. This was over the income tax issue. South Pacific Brewery Ltd. was fortunate indeed to gain the services as director, of so outstanding a figure as Jimmy James.

During 1956, the position of the company steadily improved. In the 1956/57 financial year, beer production exceeded 300,000 gallons — less than half the amount imported, but a significant increase on the previous year. Beer imports remained remarkably steady during the 1950s, despite such measures as hefty shipping freight increases — to 205 shillings per ton on Australian beer in October, 1954 — increased duty, and import restrictions imposed by the Australian Government at intervals between 1952 and 1958, to conserve overseas exchange.

The increase in production of SP beer brought with it a problem: that of finding additional bottles. Initial supplies had been obtained in Australia, at very considerable cost: more than one shilling each, landed. How to protect the ownership of these expensive bottles had been discussed at the earliest meetings of the South Pacific board. What was sold was the content, not the container, but this distinction was a very slim one to the PNG public. And not only the public. Six months after the brewery began production, Port Moresby Freezing Co. Ltd. was offering sixpence per dozen, collected, for empty beer bottles, to be used in their soft drink manufacture. The position was the same in all major PNG centres. The company published a series of warnings against the improper use of SP bottles, which had little effect. The only way to recover a significant percentage of SP empties was to make it worth while to the beer purchaser. A deposit of four shillings was therefore charged on each carton of twelve bottles sold, refundable if returned in good condition.

There were actually millions of empty bottles in Port Moresby, but they were effectively beyond the reach of the brewery and the soft drink manufacturers. In July, 1953, J.W. Bax, a member of the newly-formed Spearfishermen's Association, went for a dive in Port Moresby harbour. Five hundred yards out from the main wharf he came across an amazing sight. 'The harbour is bottomed with about six acres of bottles lying on the sea bed,' he told a *South Pacific Post* reporter. 'It's the most astounding thing I've ever seen. Bottles of all shapes and sizes, most of them old-fashioned liquor, lemonade and beer bottles. They must have been there for years!' Bax had found the dumping-ground from the Top and Bottom pubs in the years before the Pacific war.

Late in 1957 the bottle position became serious. A good percentage of empties had always been returned for the deposit, but over the years losses had multiplied, and it once again became necessary to import new bottles from Australia, this time at a cost of ten shillings per dozen. Wooden crates were imported from Singapore at the same time, to provide greater protection for the costly bottles. SP beer now became available in crates of four dozen bottles. The price of the beer was increased by four shillings per dozen, but no bottle deposit was charged. In full page advertisements in the local newspaper, the company pleaded with consumers to help preserve the 'Bottle Cycle' by returning empty bottles, promising to buy back any quantity for four shillings per dozen. A subsidiary company, Moresby Bottle Co. Ltd., was established to look after the collection of empties.

Although 1956 was a good year for South Pacific Brewery Ltd., it was no time for the company to rest on its laurels. To effectively counter the competition from imported beers, the production capacity of the brewery had yet again to be increased, and during 1956, with the newly-gained technical advice of the Heineken Group, an ambitious plan of expansion designed to at least double output was drawn up. Negotiations were undertaken with Port Moresby Freezing Co. and Burns Philp for additional land, and Pacific Holdings Ltd. agreed to provide a loan of £120,000 at 5½ per

SP Brewery prior to the 1957 extensions.

Equipment being transported to the brewery for the first major exhibition, 1957.

cent to finance the extensions. Work began in 1957. It was none too soon, for in this year a rival brewery was established, at Lae.

On 2 January, 1957, Rudolf Meier resigned as general manager of South Pacific Brewery Ltd. He was replaced by W.H.Johns. The sales manager, J.R.Nydam, also resigned. Soon afterwards it was common knowledge that a brewing company was being formed in Lae by Meier, Nydam, R.F.Bunting, L.E.Ashton, Mrs Flo Stewart and others. In June, a public statement was made by the well-known Port Moresby solicitor, Craig Kirke, who was a director of the new company, Guinea Brewery Ltd. 'We hope to produce our first trial batch of beer by Christmas,' said Kirke. 'Work on the brewery has started. The office block has been built and some of the fresh water tanks have been completed. We intend using rainwater for our beer, because the water from the Markham River is too dirty. Our production capacity will be 500,000 gallons per year, eventually.'

In October, Rudolf Meier announced that half of the expected £100,000 cost of the first stage of the new brewery had been spent, with the project 75 per cent complete. Five concrete rainwater tanks, each holding 6,000 gallons, would be fed from the 23,000 square feet catchment area of the main and office buildings. It was calculated that one inch of rain would supply 150,000 gallons. Meier said that each gallon of beer required four gallons of water to produce, but that he did not anticipate any difficulty with water supplies. Lae's average annual rainfall was more than 200 inches (compared with the beggarly forty inches of Port Moresby). Guinea Brewery Ltd. would be marketing their product in new eighteen-gallon stainless steel kegs, and in twenty-six ounce bottles.

The Guinea Brewery challenge was the biggest problem facing the newly appointed manager of South Pacific Brewery Ltd., William Henry Johns.

Born in 1912 at Broken Hill, New South Wales, Bill Johns came to the Mandated Territory of New Guinea in 1931, one of the thousands of young men lured by the glittering promise of the Morobe Goldfield. Quickly disillusioned by his failure to find gold, he got a job with Bulolo Gold Dredging Ltd. as a fitter's assistant on the Number Four dredge, and later he took over the company store at Bulwa, managing it until the outbreak of the war with Japan. He joined the New Guinea Volunteer Rifles, and as a warrant officer ran carrier-lines for the Army between Wau, Salamaua and Lae. When the NGVR was disbanded, Bill Johns followed Jim Cromie, Joe Bourke and other Goldfield identities into ANGAU, where he was promoted to the rank of lieutenant.

In 1943, Johns was seconded to the Production Control Board, then chaired by Brigadier D.M.Cleland, who in 1953 was to become Administrator of Papua New Guinea. 'Our job was to rehabilitate plantations and industry,' Johns said in an interview many years later, 'and look after the interests of Europeans who would be returning after the war. We helped them re-establish, and set up supply lines for them.'

Sir Donald Cleland.

36

The war over, Bill Johns returned to Broken Hill, where his father was licencee of the South Australian Hotel. He took over the hotel and ran it until 1951. Although he came from a family of publicans, Johns could not settle down to the life of a hotelier in the far west of New South Wales. The contrast with his old life in New Guinea was too great. He sold the South Australian Hotel, and in 1952 went back to PNG as manager of the Burns Philp subsidiary, Port Moresby Freezing Co. Ltd. His expert knowledge of the hotel trade was invaluable, since PMF ran the Moresby and Papua Hotels. When Rudolf Meier resigned, Bill Johns was offered the job of manager of South Pacific Brewery Ltd., initially for a period of two years. He accepted. He was to remain manager, then general manager and finally a director of the company until his death, in January 1982.

Bill Johns took up his appointment on 1 August, 1957. At a meeting of the board held a week later, the extent of his authority was clearly outlined. He was 'responsible for the general administration of the brewery under the guidance of the board'. His duties would cover 'sales promotion, including advertising, all staff problems such as remuneration, general conditions of service and accommodation, all correspondence, accounts, and the general administration of the day to day running of the brewery'.

Rudolf Meier had been both brewmaster and general manager, but the affairs of South Pacific Brewery Ltd. were now too complex for the perpetuation of such a dual role. A Malayan Breweries brewer, Ludwig Schilling, had been appointed assistant to Meier after the MBL takeover; he now became brewmaster, assisted by Bruce Flynn, who had joined the company in January, 1955, and who was to become general manager on the retirement of Bill Johns in 1973.

5

Fluctuating Fortunes

Guinea Brewery beer came on the market in mid-1958. By December, South Pacific Brewery was beginning to feel the pinch of competition. It was an unfortunate time for Bill Johns to have begun his new career, for the next few years were to see declining profits, rising costs and a renewed onslaught on the PNG market by popular Australian beer brands.

The major market for SP beer when Johns took over was still Port Moresby. Prior to the opening of the rival brewery, Lae, too, had been an expanding market but little growth could now be expected there — indeed, the company would do well to hold the market share it had already won. Rabaul was not at this time a significant consumer of SP. The majority of the town's drinkers preferred Australian beer. Imported beer outsold the local product in most other PNG centres.

Soon after taking up his new position, Bill Johns toured PNG, examining the marketing arrangements for SP beer in each district. He quickly came to the conclusion that SP would never achieve the desired Territory-wide sales unless the existing, somewhat haphazard marketing methods were improved. On his return he reported to the board that it was essential to establish adequate storage facilities in each main coastal centre.

Suitable local agents must be appointed to control storage, distribution and servicing of equipment. While draught beer sales in major centres were most important, the needs of outlying areas had to be met by ensuring the availability of adequate supplies of bottled beer. The board instructed Johns to prepare and implement a national marketing plan.

Expansion of the production capacity of the brewery continued. Architect J.R.Wild was appointed to supervise new building construction. There were staff increases too, both European and Papua New Guinean. Roy McKain had joined the company in 1953, as a clerk; he was to remain with South Pacific Brewery Ltd., until his retirement in 1980. A staff provident fund and superannuation plan was developed. More staff created a need for more costly accommodation, a perennial source of difficulty and frustration in Port Moresby (and all other major PNG centres). It was a problem that few organisations were able to fully overcome.

The question of bottle supplies still plagued Bill Johns and his team. The public responded well to the 'Bottle Cycle' plea of late 1957 and bottle stocks gradually increased, but it was a continuing battle to maintain them at a safe level. The possibility of obtaining used bottles from Cairns and Townsville and other towns in North Queensland was studied at board meetings. Joe Bourke, still a director, suggested that the obvious solution to the bottle problem was to manufacture them locally. (Bourke was a far-sighted man — in 1970, Australian Consolidated Industries commenced to manufacture bottles in a modern factory at Lae.)

Late in 1958, Victoria Bitter beer was released on the PNG market — in cans. This was the first time Australian beer had been made available in

Above *The brewery in 1967 after major extensions;* left, *further extensions resulted in a new two-storey office block.*

39

cans, and the new pack was immediately popular with the PNG consumer. Beer in light, tough, easily chilled cans was far cheaper to transport by air than the bottled product, and appealed strongly to the outstation drinker.

The appearance of Australian canned beer posed an obvious threat to the market position of South Pacific Brewery Ltd., and at a meeting of the board in September, 1958, a proposal by MBL to install a canning line was discussed. In the complete absence of cost estimates, no decision could be reached.

At the same meeting, Joe Bourke — who now lived outside Bulolo, where he had set up a small soft drink factory — advised that Guinea Brewery Ltd. was beginning to make considerable inroads into the company's sales in the Morobe District, with promises of a free gas service to retailers, and free transportation of beer. This was of particular concern to Joe Bourke. As an SPB shareholder, he naturally wanted to see increased sales of the company's beer. Moreover, in 1955 he had founded the Morobe Hotels Ltd. group (currently owning the Goroka, Cecil and Wau Hotels) and by arrangement with the board was paid a special commission on all SP beer sales in Wau and Bulolo. This amounted to a considerable sum — £2,501 for the nineteen months from March, 1959, to November, 1960, alone — and Joe wanted to protect this income. He suggested that the board look at the possibility of purchasing a controlling interest in Guinea Brewery Ltd., but no action was taken.

The annual report for the year ending 28 February, 1959, did not make heartening reading for the shareholders of South Pacific Brewery Ltd. What was accurately described as 'severe competition' from Australian canned beer — a number of brands were now on the market — together with Guinea Brewery sales, the cost of servicing the recently increased loan by Pacific Holdings Ltd. for the brewery extensions, and rising maintenance, raw materials and container costs, resulted in a reduction of profit after depreciation from £22,465 in 1958 (when a 10 per cent dividend was paid) to £5,101. Only the sizeable balance of £31,000 carried forward from the previous year allowed the payment of a 5 per cent dividend.

Chairman J.I.Cromie had some happier news for shareholders. Pacific Holdings had agreed to lower the interest on their loan from 5½ to 4 per cent and to raise additional funds to reduce the loan, the company was offering 150,000 new shares in the proportion of one share for every share held. New import duties imposed by the Administration on Australian and foreign beers could be expected to increase consumption of the local product. However, Cromie warned, 'in the opinion of the board it will take some time before the company can expect to increase its profits to a reasonable level as a result of the planned reorganisation of the marketing of the company's products'.

Bill Johns was making solid progress with his national marketing plan, but the desired results could not be achieved overnight. In the sixteen months ending 30 June, 1960,[1] South Pacific Brewery Ltd. made a loss of £7,059. No dividend was paid. The following year saw a slight recovery to a profit of £11,572, but again no dividend was recommended. But sales were now on the increase and the brewery extensions had been completed. Beer production rose from 320,000 gallons in 1959/60 to 411,000 gallons in 1961/62, and to 656,000 gallons the following year. The net profit in 1961/62 was £32,786, and a 5 per cent dividend was paid. The corner had been turned by 30 June, 1963. Profit was up to £76,741, and the dividend was 10 per cent.

Of course, competition from imported beer over this period also affected the opposition company, Guinea Brewery Ltd. Production at the Lae brewery rose from 72,000 gallons in 1958/59 to 153,000 gallons in 1960/61, and declined by 21,000 gallons the following year. Joe Bourke informed the board that he had talked to Rudolf Meier, who was 'very depressed', and was obviously angling to see if there was any possibility of disposing of his interest in Guinea Brewery Ltd. to South Pacific Brewery.

Despite the rapid increase in production of SP beer, imports still held the major share of the market. In 1962/63, imports jumped from 532,500 gallons the previous year to 824,600 gallons, a peak figure that was not again approached for the rest of that decade. But local beer production was about to explode, for in November, 1962, an event of enormous significance to the brewing industry, and to the nation, occurred: Papua New Guineans gained the right to drink.

1 The company had changed to a conventional financial year, ending 30 June.

The Abolition of Prohibition

When Joe Bourke and Tom Yeomans formed their Brewery Syndicate in 1950, the possibility that one day Papua New Guineans would be allowed to consume the product they hoped to brew had never crossed their minds. From the beginning of white settlement, the people had been forbidden alcohol for their own protection, and in 1950 few whites — or, for that matter, Papua New Guineans — expected that this position would change.

The first ordinance ever passed in British New Guinea, No. 1 of 1888, prohibited the supply to the native people of firearms, liquor and opium. When Australia took over responsibility for the administration of the Territory, now called Papua, prohibition for the people was continued as a matter of basic policy. Between 1901 and 1905, a vigorous campaign was waged by an influential lobby in the Australian Parliament to introduce total prohibition in Papua. The move was defeated with the support of such leading missionaries as W.E.Bromilow, Copland King and C.W.Abel, mainly on the grounds that prohibition would be an arbitrary interference with reasonable liberty — of the white man.

The Germans prohibited the supply of alcoholic liquor to the native inhabitants of German New Guinea, although restricted liquor permits were introduced in 1909. Under the terms of the Mandate given to Australia by the League of Nations in 1920, alcohol was denied to the people of New Guinea. The *Papua and New Guinea Act*, 1949, of the Australian Parliament continued this prohibition, 'subject to such exceptions and exemptions as are provided by ordinance'.

When South Pacific Brewery began to produce beer in November, 1952, informed opinion in PNG was still in favour of total prohibition for the native people, but as the years went by the position began to change, slowly at first but then with increasing rapidity. By the middle of the decade, the legal prohibition of alcoholic drink was seen by many Papua New Guineans to be a deliberate act of racial discrimination, not protection. Prohibition came to be the most bitterly resented of all the discriminatory measures still in force in PNG.

Change was slow to begin, and was dogged by controversy and argument along the way. In 1946, a liquor ordinance confirmed total prohibition in both Papua and the Territory of New Guinea. The *Liquor Ordinance* 1948 allowed selected mixed race persons to be issued with permits to drink under carefully defined circumstances. In 1950, the *Arms, Liquor and Opium Prohibition Ordinances* of Papua and New Guinea were amended to allow Papua New Guineans to consume sacramental wine in a recognised religious service. Denied normal alcoholic drink, some Papua New Guineans turned to methylated spirits, wood alcohol and similar dangerous substitutes. In the early 1950s consumption of methylated spirits began to rise alarmingly. In Port Moresby, where the position was most serious, District Commissioner M.J.Healy came to an informal agreement with local traders to limit spirits sales, but this of course had no legal force. To introduce some measure of legal control, the *Native Administration Regulations* were amended to allow Papua New Guineans to be in possession of methylated spirits only if holding a permit from a District Commissioner or his delegate. A 'crime wave' was reported in Port Moresby. Native people, some of them looking for liquor, committed no less than eight robberies in a period of three months!

Illicit consumption of alcohol by a small minority of Papua New Guineans living in and around the larger towns — in particular, Port Moresby and Rabaul — was not uncommon before the Pacific war, and certainly increased after the conflict. The Motu peoples came into contact with servicemen from Australia and America during the war, and undoubtedly obtained from them small supplies of alcohol. The Tolai learned to distil crude spirits from the Japanese during the occupation of the Gazelle, and many a village had its rough still. As early as 1946, sixty-nine villagers were arrested and forty-nine convicted of drunken behaviour during the opening of a new church near Kokopo, and in 1947 eleven men from Vunamami died after drinking spirits from a drum survivors said they had found in the bush. During 1948, a total of 158 Papua New Guineans were convicted in the courts of drinking offences; in 1954 the number had risen to 313. All told, 1,857 convictions were recorded between 1948 and 1954, a very small percentage of the total population, but significant nevertheless.

In the early post-war years, the liquor laws allowed magistrates to fine native offenders up to £30, in default imprisonment for up to six months. In February, 1952, the Central District Advisory Council recommended an amendment to the legislation, to allow magistrates to sentence offenders to gaol without the option of a fine.

The Administration allowed the amendment, but native drinking continued to increase, despite severe sentences. Offenders generally went to gaol, usually for six months. In Rabaul, a Tolai taxi driver offered to transport a passenger for beer, rather than money. Unfortunately for him, the passenger happened to be Magistrate R.G.Ormsby. The taxi driver went to gaol for four months. In the same session, Ormsby gaoled four other Tolai convicted of drinking for six months each. These were typical sentences, applying in all Territory town courts.

Suppliers of alcohol to Papua New Guineans were also hit heavily by the courts. A European was gaoled in Port Moresby in August, 1952, for six months. Soon afterwards, a Chinese woman storekeeper in Rabaul was imprisoned for six months for selling a bottle of rum to a Tolai. In September, 1954, Magistrate J.R.Rigby sent Lam Cheong (an eighty-four year old Chinese who had lived in Rabaul for fifty-eight years) to gaol for three months for supplying liquor to a native; another Chinese, sixty-five years old, was gaoled for twelve months on two charges.

These were heavy sentences, and leading Papua New Guineans began, hesitantly at first, to voice their resentment. Aisoli Salin, nominated member for the New Guinea Islands, spoke in the Legislative Council in November, 1953:-

'Liquor was never known before the Europeans came here. You taught the natives to drink...the people are drinking in every district. I am not trying to hide this...if half-castes can drink, why not allow long-service natives, members of the Police, and intelligent natives to drink?' The permit system, allowing mixed race people to consume alcohol, was a sore point with many Papua New Guineans.

The Administration was well aware of the invidiousness of the existing legal position. In February, 1952, official member J.K.McCarthy spoke in the Legislative Council on the need for reform of the liquor laws. 'There are both injustice and insult toward some classes of people in the present law,' said McCarthy. 'As the Territory grows in importance, visits of prominent persons, persons of other than European descent, might be anticipated. As the law stands, it would be an offence to offer them hospitality.' As the law stood, it was an offence to give Aisoli Salin and the other native members of the Council, a drink!

An illustration of the problems facing the small, emerging educated minority of Papua New Guineans was afforded in April, 1954. Collis Cain and Frank Aisi, two of the first Assistant Medical Practitioners to be trained for the Public Health Department at the Central Medical School in Suva, Fiji, were charged at Port Moresby with drinking alcohol. Appearing on their behalf, the Director of Public Health, Dr. John Gunther — out-spoken in his support for liquor law reform — pointed out that the two young defendants were people in transition, standard-bearers for their race. They had been sent to Suva by the Administration and thus exposed to a situaton where they were in constant contact with people from other Pacific territories who drank. Now they faced gaol for doing the same thing in their homeland. The magistrate accepted Gunther's case and imposed nominal fines of one pound each.

The editor of the *South Pacific Post* — which was for sensible liquor reform — applauded the decision, and condemned the 'small section of the public' blindly opposed to all native drinking, in particular the Christian

Missions.

Those against all native drinking were in fact far from being a 'small section' of the white population in the early 1950s. When the Legislative Council passed a Bill in November 1953, still prohibiting the supply of liquor to natives but including a section (Section 8) giving the Administrator, personally, the power to grant permits to drink to selected individuals, there was a lengthy, often heated debate. Mission members, predictably, opposed Section 8, but so did elected members such as Don Barrett. The Bill was passed, but only because the Administration had the numbers. The Administrator, D.M.Cleland, was personally convinced that reform had to come, a view shared by most — but not all — official members of the Council.

Although passed by the Council, the permit scheme was rejected by Canberra. This decision was bitterly received by educated Papua New Guineans. The *South Pacific Post* 'deplored the overriding of yet another piece of legislation passed by the Legislative Council. The Administrator, who alone would issue permits, surely could be trusted to use his power with extreme caution and discretion? To carry on under the existing archaic laws is to invite trouble, and throw up a barrier before the handful of natives who have all but succeeded in attaining a European way of life'.

Another Bill went before the Council in March, 1955, again giving the Administrator the right to allow 'chosen natives' to drink. The Bill provided for the appointment of a Liquor Consent Board, composed of the Director of District Services and Native Affairs, the Director of Public Health and the Commissioner of Police, who would make recommendations to the Administrator. Again the non-official members objected. The well-respected B.E.Fairfax-Ross asked for the measure to be deferred for five years.

Unwilling to force the Bill through the Council, the Administrator adjourned the hearing. But, he warned, 'the subject must sooner or later be faced'. A Select Committee of the Council was set up to examine the whole question. As the debate proceeded, THE DRUM column in the *South Pacific Post* was informing readers that an estimated 80 per cent of all Hanuabada men, and 20 per cent of all Papua New Guinean men living in Port Moresby, were drinking alcohol, mainly rum, gin and whisky.

Liquor for natives was becoming a talking-point throughout PNG. A typical letter in the *South Pacific Post* commented that 'the lowest grade "non native" scalawags and flotsam of the Pacific can drink themselves silly every night, subject only to the laws regarding disorderly behaviour...any rubbish from overseas is regarded as superior to our local natives. The natives believe this...'. On the other hand, ex-Sergeant-Major Topedic, a Tolai war hero, warned that grave trouble would follow if drink permits were introduced. He himself had served five gaol terms each of six months for drinking, so he knew what he was talking about!

Most public bodies throughout PNG firmly opposed the liquor permit scheme. The Lae, Kokopo, Rabaul, Madang and Port Moresby Town

Advisory Councils came out in favour of prohibition. The Rabaul branch of the Returned Servicemen's League 'deplored' Cleland's lack of support of prohibition, and this opposition was later endorsed by the RSL territorial headquarters. The President of the Bougainville Association handed Brigadier Cleland a strong letter of protest, signed by such noted figures as Paul Mason and Fred Archer.

The Select Committee toured PNG, taking evidence on the liquor issue. Dr John Gunther, a member, withdrew on the grounds that his feelings were well-known, and he did not want the public to think that he was influencing the outcome. His place was taken by R.F.Bunting. The other members were Fr. J. Dwyer, Rev. D.E.Ure, T.Grahamslaw and J.K. McCarthy. Of these, Dwyer and Ure had already publicly supported prohibition, while McCarthy was for reform.

The Select Committee delivered its report in October, 1955. It recommended the repeal of the March, 1955, legislation giving the Administrator the power to issue permits to drink, and the setting up of machinery to allow very carefully selected Papua New Guineans to receive permits, in three year's time. In the meantime, the Administration, the Missions and other interested bodies should combine to educate the people on the use and abuse of alcohol. During this period, the 'strongest possible action' should be taken to eradicate illicit drinking. The Committee recognised the existence of a demand for drink, but said it was confined in the main to the 'new middle class, in close contact with Europeans, often in better than average jobs, more intelligent and better schooled'.

The report was adopted, and the legislation was repealed. Educated Papua New Guineans were dissatisfied, and those against liquor reform were dissatisfied, too, seeing the new arrangements as the thin edge of the wedge. The doughty Australian temperance champion, Rev. Alan Walker — on a tour of PNG — said that total prohibition was the only answer. 'It is unworthy and unchristian for Europeans to demand liquor when it obviously will carry great destructiveness to native society.' Crocodile shooter Tom Cole and hotel keeper Peter England — no teetotallers, they — hotly rebutted the argument. And indeed there was no chance that total prohibition would ever have been accepted in PNG.

The courts continued to imprison and fine Papua New Guineans for drinking, and their suppliers. The demand for the right to drink increased. In a meeting with the people of Hanuabada, the visiting Minister for Territories, Paul Hasluck, was asked when the government was going to allow them to drink. Local government councillors at the meeting openly told the Minister they were drinking already. District Commissioner Alan Timperley admitted that drinking in Hanuabada was 'prevalent. We, and the police, have tried hard for months to find where the native gets his drink', he said.

The drink issue remained unresolved, a constant source of friction and bitterness among the growing class of educated Papua New Guineans who considered they had earned the right to consume alcohol. Sensational events like the lurid double murders at Rabaul (Adele Woo and Leo Wattemena, killed in May, 1956, and Carol Wright — an Australian girl, only sixteen years old — and her Chinese boyfriend, Daniel Ng, in January, 1957) grabbed the headlines, temporarily, but the question of drink for the people was never absent for long from newspaper pages.

In July, 1957, four of the first group of Papua New Guinean students to be sent to Australia for secondary schooling were sent back to the Territory for drunkenness and misbehaviour. They had been accommodated away from the school — at Charters Towers, Queensland — at a hostel, and had been given drink by other residents. The Administration terminated their scholarships and announced that future students would be boarders. The plight of the four — who were given Public Service jobs on their return — attracted wide sympathy in PNG, and again there were calls for a change in the liquor laws.

In Port Moresby the position was becoming serious. In the last three months of 1957, fifty-five Papua New Guineans were convicted on various liquor charges. Then, in August, 1959, the sort of tragedy that many observers had been predicting would occur if the people were not allowed to drink, did occur. Ironically, South Pacific Brewery Ltd. was indirectly involved.

On 3 August, Madu Pame, an apprentice electrician at the Brewery, took home a quantity of methanol, a form of alcohol used as a refrigerant. He threw a party for a group of his friends. During the wild night of drinking that followed, Madu Pame and five others died, and two more were blinded. Bill Johns acted swiftly to ensure that no further thefts of methanol from the Brewery could happen, but nothing could reduce the dimensions of the terrible event. There was a storm of protest in Port Moresby. Papuan leaders warned that more people would die if the drinking laws were not changed. Hundreds of Papua New Guineans signed a petition asking for the whole liquor question to be reopened. District Officer David Marsh confirmed that 'all natives in Port Moresby are talking about the six liquor deaths — those who died are now considered martyrs to the cause'. Brigadier Cleland announced that the liquor question would 'probably be reopened'.

In October, 1959, Fr. J.Dwyer told the Legislative Council that there was a £52,000 liquor racket operating in Rabaul. In an effort to curb the drinking of methylated spirits, the Administration had earlier that year placed restrictions on the import of spirits, and Tolai drinkers were forced to turn to black-market gin, rum and brandy. There had been an increase of 35,000 bottles of these spirits imported to Rabaul in the past three months, compared with the three months preceeding the import restrictions. Dwyer charged that the whole of this increase was going to the native people. 'Practically all the abuses have stemmed from the operations and greed of a small number of Rabaul shopkeepers,' he said.

From the beginning of the liquor debate in the early 1950s the position of the Christian Missions had been quite clear. The annual Conferences of the Missions consistently opposed drink for Papua New Guineans, principally on moral and religious grounds. The chief Roman Catholic delegate to the Fourth Conference in 1952, Bishop Wade, summed up the feelings of missionaries of all denominations in the words, 'I would not consider for a moment the right of anyone to give a native strong drink'.

The next Conference was not held until November, 1954. During his speech at the opening ceremony, Brigadier Cleland urged the delegates to debate the question of native drink permits and made his position plain. 'It is my own conviction after careful consideration and observation that we cannot and must not stand resolutely and, in the long run, perhaps unwisely, on the plank of total prohibition,' he said. 'We cannot on the one hand advocate the advancement of the native in all important aspects of his life...and then, on the other hand, say to him, "you shall not do the things we do". We are storing up the ingredients for the future of a situation which would in the ultimate be far worse in its consequences than any which might arise now under a system of exemptions wisely, and very carefully, administered. Clear and definite action is required today, not tomorrow.' Despite his arguments, the Conference again endorsed prohibition.

The united front of the Christian Missions appeared to crack, slightly, in 1955. Bishop Leo Sharmach of Rabaul said in April that he favoured the use of liquor permits to 'certain sections of the educated community. I particularly refer to our native priests. They live with us, and eat with us'. However, the secretary of the Methodist Overseas Mission, Rabaul, was quick to reaffirm the opposition of his church. The Missions Conferences in 1957 and 1959 once more were united on the question of prohibition for Papua New Guineans.

By 1961, however, not even the stoutest Mission supporter of prohibition could deny that a crisis point was fast approaching. The resentment of Papua New Guineans of what they saw to be liquor laws based solely upon race, knew no bounds. National leaders were emerging in ever-increasing numbers, and they were demanding action.

At the 1961 Conference, a historic resolution was passed:-

'With the development of the people towards self-determination, this Conference is of the opinion that on principle such determination should also be extended to measures introduced for their protection, and which are now deemed to be discriminatory.

'Therefore, it recommends that any change in the present laws covering the use of liquor by the indigenous people should only be decided by the will of the people.

'This should be expressed through some form of local option, and be covered by adequate safeguards. It further recommends that before the will of the people is sought in this matter, the Administration, through its own services, should undertake an educational campaign on what alcohol is, and what it does.'

The resolution, drawn up by representatives of the Unevangelised Fields Mission, Methodist Overseas Mission, Seventh Day Adventist

Mission, London Missionary Society, and the Anglican and Franciscan Missions, was passed unanimously, after long debate.

This change of heart by the moral and spiritual guardians of the Papua New Guinea people marked a decisive turning-point in the battle to overthrow the hated prohibition. Of course, the Missions were merely choosing what they saw to be the lesser of two evils, racial discrimination or liquor, but their resolution carried a great deal of weight, and smoothed the way for a political decision to lift prohibition. Shortly afterwards the Council of Social Services — set up to bring together representatives of the various bodies doing social work in the Port Moresby area — appointed a subcommittee to examine the question. Its report, too, favoured a relaxation of prohibition:-

'As matters rest, the continuing prohibition on native drinking is promoting contempt for the law generally, and is breeding political resentment. If we, as Australians, are supposed to be leading the people of this country on the road to equal partnership and equal responsibility, it seems to the subcommittee that we can no longer treat them as children, and deny them the beginnings of equality, whether they abuse the privilege at first or not.'

Brigadier Cleland now acted. The Minister for Territories, Paul Hasluck, had left the whole prohibition question up to him. 'In conversations with the Administrator,' Hasluck wrote in his 1976 book, *A Time For Building*, 'I said that the responsibility lay on him to watch the local situation and to make whatever recommendations he thought the situation required. In a matter depending so much on a judgement on local conditions, I would not move without his recommendation, and would hold off pressures for change as long as he thought I should do so.' On 12 February, 1962, Cleland recommended to Hasluck that it was now time to relax the law of total prohibition. An independent Commission should be set up to advise on the means and methods of doing this. Hasluck took the recommendation to Federal Cabinet — the move might be expected to attract political opposition — which approved the setting up of the Commission.

On 23 July, 1962, Cleland appointed a Committee of Inquiry, headed by F.R.Nelson, a Victorian judge, and including as members R.G.Ormsby, magistrate; Stanis Boramilat, a Tolai councillor; Reverend Percy Chatterton, LMS missionary; Mase Rei, a Papuan automotive salesman and councillor; Father John O'Hanlan, Roman Catholic missionary, and social worker Mrs Thelma Price. No representative of the hotel or liquor industries was appointed. The President of the Papua and New Guinea Hotels Association, Wally Morrissey, complained to the Minister, but the membership was not altered.

The Committee was not set up to advise whether or not Papua New Guineans should be allowed to drink, Cleland announced — that decision had already been made. 'Its task will be to advise on ways and means of changing the present law.'

Indeed the time was overdue for change. In January, 1962, Hasluck had visited PNG on one of his last tours as Minister, and was everywhere faced with demands by local leaders and councillors for the right to drink. He publicly acknowledged — for the first time — the need for reform, and for this was applauded by the editor of the *South Pacific Post*. Reform was 'without doubt the most important question exercising the minds of thinking people in the Territory today,' said the editor. Native drinking had just been introduced, uneventfully, in the British Solomon Islands Protectorate, which increased the pressure for change.

Reform, generally, of PNG law to remove racial discrimination was already under way. Begun on the direct instructions of Paul Hasluck, progress in the work was at first very slow, but in March, 1962, the first Bill — to repeal the *Native Women's Protection Ordinance* — was brought before the Legislative Council.

The issue of racial discrimination in PNG came sharply into focus in January, 1962. Julius Chan, a young mixed race Native Affairs officer, had applied for membership of the Konedobu Club, whose membership was mainly drawn from Public Service circles. He was nominated for membership by the Director of Native Affairs, J.K.McCarthy. Despite this, the Club Committee rejected Chan's application, whereupon McCarthy resigned from the Club. Fifteen members signed a petition seeking a reversal of the Committee's decision, and calling for the club to be opened to all, 'regardless of race, colour and creed'. On 30 March the Committee once again rejected Chan's application, and the move to open membership. Two more influential Club members — C.J.Lynch, the Chief Legislative Draftsman, and R.Thomson, a senior Native Affairs officer — resigned. The Konedobu Club was in turmoil.

The affair was front page news, and was discussed all over PNG. 'It is a fair assumption to make that the Konedobu Club is for Europeans only,' said the editor of the *South Pacific Post*. This was undoubtedly true. (Sir Julius Chan later became a Prime Minister of Papua New Guinea, and the Konedobu Club now admits members 'regardless of race, colour or creed'.)

The Territory-wide debate on the Chan affair was at its height when the 1962 Visiting Mission of the United Nations came to PNG, in April. Led by Sir Hugh Foot, this Mission was certainly the most influential of all the United Nations Missions to PNG. The Report of the Mission urged Australia to force the pace of development — political, economic and social — in PNG; to urgently prepare the people for self-government and independence. It recommended the establishment of a university, the strengthening of the economy, and the replacement of the Legislative Council by a new body, with a membership of 100, mainly elected from a common roll.

Wherever the Foot Mission went in PNG, it met with demands from the people for the right to drink. Earlier Missions had faced similar requests, but now the question was given extraordinary prominence at almost every meeting the Mission had with the people. The decision to abandon prohibition had already been made when the Foot Mission arrived in PNG, but certainly the report of the Mission — which 'welcomed the government's action' — helped to speed proceedings. 'It is humiliating to be denied alcoholic drink at social gatherings and joint receptions of the kind attended in many places by the Mission', said the report. 'The time has come to sweep away all survivals of racial discrimination...'.

It was in this climate of impending change that the Committee of Inquiry began its task. The terms of reference were to inquire into and report upon, firstly, 'the means and methods by which the law of total prohibition on the consumption of intoxicating liquor by natives may be relaxed', and, secondly, 'to examine the present liquor laws in the Territory and to recommend a comprehensive liquor and licencing Ordinance to provide for, *inter alia*,

(a) the establishment of a single Licensing Commission;
(b) adequate machinery to carry out the means and methods of relaxation of the total prohibition of the consumption of intoxicating liquor by natives;
(c) adequate penalties for breaches of the law relating to intoxicating liquor, and
(d) stricter control over the supply and sale of intoxicating liquor generally'.

This Commission acted so promptly and reported so swiftly that it established something of a record for government inquiries of this magnitude, before or since. Appointed on 23 July, 1962, it commenced its work on 9 August and presented its final report to the Administrator on 11 October. More than 300 persons, European and Papua New Guinean, gave evidence.

Accepting that the discrimination in race involved in total prohibition for the people was breeding resentment and a contempt for the law, the Committee recommended that 'the relaxation of the present law should be made swiftly, and before its more damaging effects grow to more serious proportions'. It recommended the drafting of a new Liquor Ordinance providing, among other measures, for the setting up of a licensing authority. In the meantime, immediate legislation should be enacted to provide during the transitory period, a modified form of relaxation of the existing laws, to allow Papua New Guineans to consume any form of alcoholic drink on licenced premises, and to purchase beer only for removal from licenced premises.

The Report of the Committee was accepted. Again in an extraordinary display (for government) of precipitate action, the *Liquor (Special Provisions) Bill* was passed on 16 October by the Legislative Council. It allowed for a relaxation of the laws as recommended by the Committee of Inquiry, and placed a total ban on all liquor advertising.

On 30 October, 1962, Joe Bourke[1] and his wife, Billie, 'went finish', leaving Papua New Guinea to settle on a small farm in Queensland. On 2 November, the new Ordinance came into effect, and prohibition for Papua New Guineans was at last ended.

1 Bourke died in Nambour, Queensland, in 1976.

7

Takeover

The *Liquor (Special Provisions) Ordinance* came into force at midnight. All Papua New Guineans over the age of eighteen years were now entitled to consume the alcoholic drinks of their choice on licenced premises, and in the towns it seemed as though everyone was determined to do so. When the hotels of the Territory opened for business on 2 November, they were rushed.

Despite the many earlier recommendations that the people should be educated in the use and abuse of alcohol before prohibition ended, very little had in fact been done. On the eve of 'D Day', as the *South Pacific Post* termed it, Dr John Gunther — who was now Assistant Administrator — pleaded with the people to 'drink sanely, observe good manners, and show consideration for other people'. The executive members of the Fairfax Local Government Council held special meetings at Hanuabada, Baruni and Tatana, and urged moderation and restraint. Similar calls were made in most districts of Papua New Guinea. A temperance society called SEVA (Society Encouraging Voluntary Abstinence) had been hastily formed at Port Moresby, by religious and social welfare interests opposed to alcohol, but it had not had time to act before prohibition ended.

'D Day', dreaded by many observers, passed almost without incident. Banner headlines in the *South Pacific Post* on 6 November told the story: 'First Rush Over. Phew! What a Weekend!'

'Port Moresby natives on Friday and Saturday bought more than 14,000 bottles of beer and downed nearly 2,000 gallons more in bars to celebrate the introduction of legalised drinking', a reporter wrote. 'They were rowdy, but good humoured...only four Papuans were convicted of drunkenness, and reports from Rabaul, Lae and Goroka indicate the position was the same as it was in Port Moresby.

'From the moment the hotel opened on Friday, a steady stream began to fill the hotels. By midday, scores were queuing at the Moresby Hotel's new bottle shop, and by 1 p.m. nearly 200 dozen bottles of beer had been sold.

52

When work finished for the day, swarms of natives invaded both town hotels. The Moresby was forced to close its doors for a time in the late afternoon. There were scores of police on duty. At 8 p.m. there were only six Europeans drinking at the Papua Hotel, and eight at the Moresby. Drinkers were standing six deep from the bars, waving pound notes and shouting for drinks. The noise was terrific! The atmosphere was cheery, and curious Europeans were greeted with backslaps and handshakes. "Have a drink, mate," was extended by all. The traditional "taubada" was dropped for "mate". Everyone had smiles and kind words. Goilalas mixed with Keremas as rum did with whisky. By 10.30 the floors of both bars were thick with a mixture of mud and spilt beer. The police came at 11 p.m. "That's all, boys," they said, and hundreds of drinkers weaved their way home, arm in arm.

'The following morning saw the bars again crowded, but practically no Europeans drank in the two town hotels...club managers reported increased business. Features of native drinking included the numbers of cold bottles of beer lost from paper bags by natives unused to their handling, the odd mixtures requested — whisky and rum was a popular compound — and the overwhelming popularity of beer among the young men...'.

There is no doubt that legalised drinking for Papua New Guineans was a boon to South Pacific Brewery Ltd. A market of hitherto unprecedented size was suddenly opened up, and no commercial enterprise could be expected to ignore such a golden opportunity. Rightly or wrongly, the nation had decided against total prohibition (which American experience had surely proved was not practicable) and Papua New Guineans quickly showed that the alcoholic drink they wanted was beer, not the far more potent spirits.

Legalised drinking came at a time when South Pacific was already climbing out of its profits slump. Competition from imported beers was still strong — as mentioned in chapter four, imports rose to 824,000 gallons in 1962/63. Australian beer was being heavily advertised in PNG before and after 'D Day', particularly Carlton and United brands. Queensland beers — Castlemaine XXXX and Bulimba Gold Top — Cascade from Tasmania and Sydney beers were being sold, but the brands most consistently promoted were Victoria Bitter, Melbourne Bitter, Fosters Lager and Abbots Lager — dubbed 'The Best' in a typical Steamships advertisement. Moreover, the sale of Australian beers was assisted by Australian Government export incentives. After 'D Day' sales of imported beers began to fall. By 1968/69, imports were down to 355,500 gallons. SP production this year had soared to 3,006,000 gallons! This figure included the output from Guinea Brewery at Lae, for in 1965 it was taken over by South Pacific Brewery Ltd.

Guinea Brewery never did succeed in selling its beer on a Territory-wide basis. It sold well on the New Guinea mainland, but performed poorly in other areas where SP was well entrenched. At the time of the takeover the Lae brewery had an annual production capacity of some 330,000 gallons, but actual production in 1964/65 amounted to 120,000 gallons only.

After 'D Day', South Pacific Brewery flourished. Bill Johns had an enlightened theory of management, and he was able to get the best out of his people. 'The best manager is the bloke who gets his team around him and lets them have a say,' he once said. 'I have found that a man who makes decisions on his own invariably makes bad ones.' Each year saw an increase in production, and SP beer became firmly established in all major Territory centres.

In the year of the Guinea Brewery takeover, the output of SP beer for the first time exceeded one million gallons. Burns Philp began to promote SP beer, vigorously. To meet the Australian competition, the company introduced a new 13⅓ ounce, non-returnable glass bottle, dubbed the 'stubby', in 1962, which quickly became popular. (Guinea Brewery also used the glass stubby). Eventually, a breakthrough was made at Rabaul, the stronghold of Victoria Bitter and other Australian beers. Arthur Brown, owner and mine host of the Ascot Hotel, agreed to accept SP draught beer — but only if the kegs were delivered, cold and dry, all condensation being mopped up to avoid staining the cellar floor! No other customer received this tender, loving care.

During this general period, there were some changes in the staffing and direction of South Pacific Brewery Ltd. As mentioned in the previous chapter, Joe Bourke left PNG to settle in Queensland, and as a result of his departure he was obliged to resign his place on the SPB board. 'Jimmy' James and Ernie Kriewaldt also resigned, and departed. (James died soon afterwards in Brisbane, in December, 1963.) To fill the vacancies, D.E.C. (Mick) Lloyd and Max Lewis were appointed directors. Max Lewis was general manager of Malayan Breweries Ltd., and Lloyd was the general manager of Hornibrook Constructions Ltd., which had built the main cellar block at the South Pacific Brewery. Jim Cromie, Max Lewis and Mick Lloyd were to direct the affairs of the company until 1969. (Bill Johns was appointed an alternate director in 1965.)

The first auditor of South Pacific Brewery Ltd. had been Dick Davies of Lae. He resigned in 1953, and was replaced by D.J.Levy. In 1960, Don Levy sold his practice to the firm of Martyn, Lord and Fishwick, Chartered Accountants, and Raymond Lord was appointed auditor to the company. J.W.Sheppard, who became company secretary when 'Jimmy' James went, remained in the position for less than twelve months, and on his resignation H.I.Firth was appointed.

Ian Firth had come to PNG to work for New Guinea Goldfields at Wau. Later he joined John Dowling in Rabaul as his company secretary, and then accepted a South Pacific Brewery offer.

A key employee in any brewing company is, of course, the brewmaster. In 1959, on the departure of Ludwig Schilling, this position was filled by Bruce A. Flynn.

Flynn gained his early experience with the big Sydney brewing company, Tooth & Co. He joined Tooth's in 1948 and while in their employ took this diploma in Applied Chemistry at the University of NSW. He worked in a variety of fields at Tooth & Co., and finally became relieving brewer.

Flynn came to South Pacific Brewery Ltd. in 1955 as assistant brewer, just in time to benefit from the newly established relationship with the Heineken Group and Malayan Breweries. He was given further specialised training in Singapore and Holland, and was made brewmaster in 1959. In 1960, Bruce Flynn was given special leave to allow him to attend the University of Queensland, for final studies leading to an Applied Science Degree. He was relieved by a Heineken brewer, Van Dam. When South Pacific Brewery Ltd. took over Guinea Brewery in 1965, Bruce Flynn became head brewer.

Another brewer who was to stay with the company for many years arrived in 1957. Karl Thoennes, a German, was trained at the Kloster brewery, Koblenz, and the St. Pauli brewery, in Hamburg. In 1953 he migrated to Australia and four years later accepted a position with South Pacific. Thoennes, too, was sent to Holland and Singapore for further training, and after Bruce Flynn was promoted to head brewer, Karl Thoennes became brewmaster at Port Moresby.

Karl Thoennes.

South Pacific Brewery beer production rapidly increased, as that of Guinea Brewery declined, in 1963 and 1964. But the competition from imported beers, although slackening, was still formidable, more than 600,000 gallons coming in during the 1963/64 financial year. It was Guinea Brewery that was most damaged by the imports; South Pacific Brewery was actually exporting considerable quantities of beer. A cargo of over 7,000 cartons of SP worth £30,000 was sent to West New Guinea ports in February, 1963, the largest export consignment shipped by the company up to that time. SP beer had been selling in West New Guinea for the past two years, and in smaller quantities in the British Solomon Islands Protectorate, and Australia. Guinea Brewery could not sell all the beer it could brew. Clearly, the logical move was for Guinea Brewery and South Pacific to get together.

Concerned at the continuing threat to the local industry from imported beer — by this time, mostly Australian, in cans and stubbies — the Territory brewing industry sought additional protection from the Administration, and in March, 1963, the Legislative Council increased the import duty on beer entering the Territory by two shillings, bringing the rate up to nine shillings and six pence per gallon. Local breweries at this time paid excise duty of five shillings and six pence per gallon, and duty also on seals, bottles, labels and materials imported from overseas. Imported beer was now considerably more expensive than the local product, and sales continued to decline. In Port Moresby, SP sold for two shillings and three pence per glass stubby (forty-two shillings per carton) as against two shillings and eleven pence for VB or MB in similar bottles. In Lae, Guinea

Brewery retailed its Guinea Special, Bitter Ale and Draught Pilsener Beer at forty shillings per carton of 24 stubbies. As a result, imported beer was consumed almost entirely by Europeans in the clubs to which, as a class, they had retreated after 'D Day'. Papua New Guineans drank local beer, and took over the hotel bars.

Despite the impetus given to the local brewing industry by native drinking, the market position of Guinea Brewery Ltd. continued to slip. In mid-1962, Sangara Holdings Ltd. had purchased a major interest in the company, but beer production went on falling. SP was now challenging Guinea Brewery beer on its home ground. The end was in sight. The possibility of an amalgamation or merger with South Pacific Brewery began to be discussed. Finally, following extended negotiations and an examination of the Guinea Brewery operation by an independent firm of chartered accountants acceptable to both sides, the Guinea Brewery directors recommended to their shareholders that they offer their shares to South Pacific Brewery Ltd. The price offered was attractive — either twenty-three shillings cash for each Guinea Brewery share, or one SPB share for each five Guinea Brewery shares — and was generally accepted by shareholders. Sangara Holdings sold their parcel in February, 1965. A total of 90,083 Guinea Brewery shares changed hands in May, and others in August. Jim Cromie reported to South Pacific Brewery shareholders in the annual report for 1964/65:-

'Guinea Brewery is now virtually a wholly-owned subsidiary of your company. A few small parcels of shares are still outstanding, but they should be acquired in the immediate future. Needless to say, the addition of another production unit with consequent saving of freight and other economies cannot fail to be of considerable advantage to us. The board is also pleased to say that it was able to finance this operation from the company's own resources . . .'.

Quite apart from the elimination of a potentially damaging competitor, the company gained a brewery in Lae with ample land for future expansion when it acquired Guinea Brewery Ltd. SPB holdings in Port Moresby were fully developed, and additional land there would be extremely difficult, and expensive, to obtain. Moreover, Lae was an ideal location for a brewery. With the recent opening of the Highlands Highway to regular vehicular traffic, Lae had become the gateway to the Highlands Districts, home of almost half the population of PNG. The New Guinea islands — Manus, New Ireland, New Britain, Bougainville — were far more accessible from Lae than from Port Moresby.

The land that Guinea Brewery owned at Lae was undoubtedly its greatest asset. The brewery itself, while functional, was small and technically of basic standard, incapable of meeting increased demands. At the time of the South Pacific takeover, the brewmaster at Lae was Rudi Bertram, a genial young German who had been trained at the Brewer's College in Berlin, and at the Berliner Kindl brewery and the Bavari brewery, in

Rudi Bertram.

Hamburg. He migrated to Australia, and worked for Tooth & Co. in Sydney for three years before accepting an offer from Rudolf Meier to join Guinea Brewery.

Meier was anxious to return to Europe. His wife was seriously ill, and he had had enough of the brewing industry in PNG. Late in 1963, he went to Australia to look for a new brewmaster. His brother-in-law worked at Tooth & Co., and he recommended Rudi Bertram.

Rudi Bertram arrived in Lae in January, 1964, and took over from Meier, who quit Papua New Guinea. 'When I got there I had one look at the brewery and I said to myself, "God, where am I?"' Bertram said in a recent interview with the author. 'Tony Matthews, production manager at Tooth's, was a friend of Bruce Flynn's, and he knew about Guinea Brewery. He said to me, "Rudi, when you get there, you'll be doing concreting and building work." I said to him, "fair go, mate, I'm a brewer", but he was right! One of the first things I had to do was repair the concrete cellar walls, which had cracked during a *guria*. I did everything!'

Rudi Bertram, now the proprietor of a busy delicatessen in Queen Street, Brisbane, shook his head and laughed softly as he remembered his early days in Lae. 'You know, it was just a little bush brewery. There was an office, a little laboratory where we did just the standard tests, two good refrigerator compressors, nine storage tanks, three fermenting tanks, and a home made brewhouse, with concrete walls filled with wood chips. There were a couple of clapped-out trucks. All our malt was handled in bags, and we got our bottles every month or so from ACI in Brisbane.

'The only European staff were another German brewer, Walter Schroder, the engineer, Garry Jansen, and Bertie Heath. Werner Bensch came in May, 1965, just before the South Pacific takeover. Our daily output in 1964 was only about 300 cartons of beer and fifty eighteen-gallon kegs. The general public used to walk right through the brewery with cartons full of empty bottles to exchange for full ones.

'The biggest problem was water. It was a very peculiar setup for a brewery. Water is the main component of beer! There was no town water then, and all we had was rainwater. Even though Lae gets a lot of rain, the storage tanks were always running out. When the tanks were low, I'd look at the sky every day, and pray for rain. Rudi Meier had dug wells all over the place, looking for water, and when the brewery first started people used to complain about the taste. The Mobil Oil Company bulk petrol tanks were right next door and of course there was often a bit of seepage. Sometimes that beer tasted very funny! But we made do, and things always seemed to work out. And it was a nice place to work, very friendly. Lae was a good town. It was home to us, you know?'

Bertie Heath, advertising and distribution manager when Rudi Bertram joined Guinea Brewery, was an institution in Lae — indeed, he was known throughout PNG. Heath was already over seventy years of age when Bertram arrived. Short and slight, Bertie Heath — peppery of speech and

Bertie Heath, who flew the first
Royal Mail run between
Adelaide and Darwin, 1930.

kind of heart — did not look what he was; one of the pioneers of civil
aviation in Australia and New Guinea, and in his day probably the best tri-
motor pilot around.

Born at Gladstone, South Australia, in 1893, Bertie Heath enlisted in
the South Australian Light Horse in 1915 and served later as a despatch
rider before joining the Royal Flying Corps in 1917. He trained as a pilot on
B.E.2C biplanes, and flew equally fragile F.E.2B fighters and F.E.8 scouts
before going out to Palestine with a D.H.9 bomber squadron. He married in
London after the end of the war, and remained in England, flying, until
1921, when he returned to Australia with his wife, Lilian.

Bertie Heath was issued with his civilian pilot's licence — bearing the
number thirty — in 1922, and in 1923 went to Western Australia to fly tri-
motors for Major Norman Brearley's West Australian Airways. Also flying
for Brearley at that time were two pilots who were soon to achieve fame:
Charles Kingsford-Smith and Keith Anderson. In the famous 'Coffee
Royal' incident of April, 1929, the missing Kingsford-Smith and his
companions (co-pilot Charles Ulm, navigator H.A.Litchfield and radio
operator T.H.McWilliams), who had been forced down in the Kimberleys
in their Fokker tri-motor, *Southern Cross*, were found by pilot Les Holden,
later well-known in New Guinea. But it was Bertie Heath who flew in to the
stranded aviators. Keith Anderson and his navigator, Bob Hitchcock, also
went looking for Kingsford-Smith. They went down in the desert after
engine failure and perished, miserably, of thirst.

In April, 1931, Bertie Heath joined Guinea Airways Ltd., and spent the
next eleven years flying Junkers G.31 tri-motor freighters between Lae,
Bulolo and Wau. This was the heroic age of flying in New Guinea. During
1931, Guinea Airways pilots carried a far greater tonnage of freight —
mostly the prefabricated gold dredges — in their Junkers aircraft than all the
rest of the world's pilots put together. In all those years, Heath had only one

crash, in April, 1934, when a cargo of poorly-stowed drums of fuel shifted on takeoff. The Junkers was badly smashed-up, but Bertie Heath and his flight mechanic were uninjured. In September, Heath had the disconcerting experience of losing the domed cover of the long cargo hatch of his G.31 in flight. He landed safely.

When the Japanese invaded new Guinea, Bertie Heath was still flying over the Goldfield routes, the acknowledged master pilot of Guinea Airways. On Wednesday 21 January, 1942, he was at the controls of the G.31, *Paul*, flying from Lae to Bulolo. Unknown to him, he was being followed by a formation of Japanese Zero fighters. The Goldfield aircraft were not fitted with radios, and Heath had not heard the warning broadcast a short time before by a Coastwatcher. He landed at Bulolo, and minutes after he had left his cockpit the Zeros swept in with machine guns blazing, and in seconds *Paul*, and the two other veteran G.31's parked nearby, called *Peter* and *Pat*, were in flames.

It was Bertie Heath's last flight as a pilot. He was now almost fifty years of age, with over 17,000 flying hours in his logbooks. The pioneering era in aviation came to an end with the Second World War. Bertie Heath was too old for combat flying during the war — he served with the RAAF in an administrative capacity — and certainly too old for commercial flying afterwards. He returned to PNG, and in 1959, at an age when most men are long retired, he joined Guinea Brewery Ltd., at the request of the then company secretary, Dick Davies.

South Pacific Brewery Ltd. also acquired the services of a number of Papua New Guineans with the Guinea Brewery takeover. Senior of these was Jack Connolly — despite his name, a Papua New Guinean from Labubutu, near the mouth of the Markham River. Jack joined Guinea Brewery soon after the company was formed, at first working in the boiler room and later in the cellars. Married, with five children, Jack Connolly stayed on after the takeover, and at the time of writing was still employed at the Lae brewery.

'An outstanding man,' Rudi Bertram says of Connolly. 'He had no real education — I taught him to tell the time — but he had a rare quality. He was a great mediator between management and the national workers. Very sensible, very dedicated man.'

There were, of course, many Papua New Guineans who had been working for South Pacific Brewery for years at the time of the Guinea Brewery takeover. From the beginning, national staff always greatly out-numbered expatriates and although most stayed with the company for a time and then moved to other employment, some remained. One such was Iluka Waru, from Kalama village, Kerema. He began work with South Pacific Brewery Ltd. in April, 1953. A man from a simple village background, Iluka received some basic education at a Mission primary school before coming to Port Moresby to look for work.

Opportunities for Papua New Guineans in the 1950s were very limited. Education then was almost entirely in the hands of the Christian Missions — it was not until the beginning of the 1960s that the great Administration effort in education began — and although the Missions did their best, it was just about impossible for the ordinary villager to acquire an education sufficient to equip him for anything but low level employment. And so it proved for Iluka. It was hard to find a job, but eventually the brewery took him on.

Iluka's subsequent career was typical of those of other nationals with similar backgrounds who worked for South Pacific Brewery Ltd., and other companies, in those days. His first task was to stack empty bottles ready to be placed on the bottle washing machine. After a year, he was transferred to the brewhouse, and then to the cellars, where he pumped beer into the fermenting tanks. He attended the filters, filled beer kegs and washed out the beer tanks.

Iluka, and others like him, were indispensible to the successful operations of companies like South Pacific Brewery, despite their lack of formal education. Over the years, men like Iluka developed a range of simple skills, and most were devoted to the interests of the companies they served.

Most of the nationals employed by the brewery in the early years were from the Kerema district, and tended — in PNG fashion — to resent the recruitment of men from other districts. Another man from Iluka's village of Kalama joined the company in April, 1958: Hio'hi Oive. Younger than Iluka, Hio'hi succeeded in passing his standard three exams at the Mission primary school at Elema, but his first job in the South Pacific brewery was also on the bottling machine. From there he graduated to the cellar, and in 1968 was transferred to the Lae brewery. Eventually he rose to the position of foreman, in charge of thirty-two workers.

Another long-serving Kerema man was Evoa Karuka. He gained a good primary education at Sogeri before seeking his fortune in Port Moresby in 1947. His first employer was Jim Cromie, and in 1950 Evoa took a job at the Port Moresby Freezing Company. When Bill Johns became manager of PMF in 1952, Evoa was impressed by him. 'He was a nice man,' he told the author at Port Moresby in January, 1982. 'Mr Johns went to South Pacific Brewery in 1957, and in April, 1959, I followed him and went to work for the brewery, too. I was a clerk in the bottling hall, then I became a driver. I trained a lot of Kerema men as clerks for South Pacific.'

Jack Connolly, Iluka Waru, Hio'hi Oive, Evoa Karuka and their fellows were men without education or special training, men who represented the old ways in PNG. But times were fast changing. Self-government and independence for PNG seemed a world away in the 1940s and 1950s. It would not be so in the 1960s. From the early years of that decade a sense of urgency would start to be felt, by those engaged in private enterprise no less than in government. The time was rapidly approaching when Papua New Guineans of ability could aspire to higher education, and associated higher material rewards. One of the first such avenues open to young nationals was gradually developed by the Administration during the 1950s, and it is to the credit of the South Pacific Brewery management that the company was one of the first to recognise its importance. This was the native apprenticeship scheme.

Although the *Apprenticeship Ordinance* was passed in 1952, the scheme did not really begin to forge ahead until 1955, when John Hohnen, managing director of New Guinea Goldfields Ltd., was appointed chairman of the Apprenticeship Board. Initially, most private employers were loath to take part. They did not have training facilities, and some doubted the capacity of Papua New Guineans to learn trade skills. Moreover, young men with the required minimum standard of education were not easy to find. The Administration was still in the process of establishing technical schools, and there were few high schools then.

John Hohnen was personally convinced of the value of apprenticeship training for Papua New Guineans and he took up the cause with enthusiasm. By the end of the 1950s major employers on the Morobe Goldfield — particularly his own company, NGG Ltd., Bulolo Gold Dredging Ltd., and Commonwealth New Guinea Timbers Ltd. which operated the big plywood factory at Bulolo — had apprentices under indenture, and in Papua the Australasian Petroleum Co. and South Pacific Brewery Ltd. were early supporters. The apprenticeship scheme gradually spread all over PNG. By June, 1960, the enrolment at technical training schools had reached 576, and there were 270 apprentices in training. South Pacific Brewery had three apprentices in training, and in 1966 the company employed a fully qualified staff training officer, W.T.Barclay.

8

The 1971 Commission of Inquiry

The years following the takeover of Guinea Brewery saw a remarkable expansion of the operations of South Pacific Brewery Ltd. In the takeover year, the combined production of the Lae and Port Moresby breweries was 1,412,000 gallons. It reached 4,334,000 gallons in 1970/71. Output from the Port Moresby brewery remained relatively static, but Lae output soared from 120,000 gallons to 2,420,000 gallons per year.

Following the takeover, a master plan of expansion of the Lae brewery was worked out by experts of the Heineken Group in consultation with South Pacific Brewery Ltd. The plan called for an increase in production capacity in stages between 1966 and 1973, and would eventually require a total expenditure of over $8 million.[1]

The first stage of the programme, completed early in 1967, lifted annual production from 330,000 to 1 million gallons per annum. Capacity rose again, to 1.7 million gallons, in 1968, and to 2,750,000 gallons in 1970. Sales continued to increase, year by year, and late in 1970 the final stage in the master expansion plan was begun, to lift capacity to 4.4 million gallons. This work was completed in February, 1973, giving South Pacific Brewery Ltd. a total output capacity from the Lae and Port Moresby breweries of 6,750,000 gallons per annum.

The company increased profits each financial year from 1966 to 1971, and paid dividends of 20, 25, 20, 22, 35 and 35 percents respectively — remarkable figures. Bonus share issues were made in 1966 — one for three — and in 1968 — one for two — and the authorised capital of the company was increased to $2 million in 1968.

Although the SPB shareholders had no cause for complaint, by far the greatest beneficiary from the increasingly lucrative operations of the company was the Administration. Governments everywhere levy heavy

Lae Brewery.

[1] Australian decimal currency was adopted within PNG at the same time it was introduced in Australia on 14 February, 1966.

taxes on tobacco and alcohol, and PNG was no exception. Thus, in 1970/71, the net profit after tax of South Pacific Brewery Ltd. and its subsidiaries amounted to just over $1 million but the company paid almost $4 million to the Administration in excise duty and income tax.

These excellent trading results were achieved despite certain developments that affected the company's position. As earlier recounted, beer imports into PNG steadily declined over the 1960s as the fortunes of South Pacific Brewery Ltd. brightened. Imports were down to 355,000 gallons by 1968/69, but in the following year they jumped to 712,300 gallons, and then to 1.3 million. In this year — 1971/72 — SP sales declined for the first time in years, by 210,000 gallons.

This upsurge in imports was mainly caused by developments on Bougainville, rising popularity of canned beer and by an Administration increase of thirty cents per gallon in the rate of excise on local beer, which sharply reduced the retail price advantage enjoyed by South Pacific Brewery products.

The discovery of copper in commercial quantities by Conzinc Riotinto of Australia Limited on Bougainville was an event of colossal economic importance to PNG. By far the biggest industrial project yet developed in PNG — indeed, a formidable undertaking even by world standards — the Bougainville copper project involved the construction of an entire town, and major harbour, earth-moving and road works, employing thousands of people, particularly during the construction phase from 1966 to 1971. Copper production began at Panguna in 1972, and in 1974 concentrates to the value of $274 million were exported, more than half the total value of PNG exports. By the end of 1972 the operating company, Bougainville Copper Ltd., was still employing over 3,000 Papua New Guineans and almost 1,000 expatriates, well below the peak construction phase level but nevertheless a large, and well paid, work force.

Beer filtration plant, Lae Brewery.

The Bougainville copper project was, from the outset, an international operation, with most of the capital and expertise coming from outside PNG. The rich Bougainville market proved to be a tough one for South Pacific Brewery Ltd. to crack. The company had an agent in Bougainville and sold a moderate amount of beer there long before the copper project began, but Bougainville Copper Ltd. showed little interest in obtaining their requirements from local suppliers. Instead, entire container loads were shipped in from overseas, including lots of Australian beer — mostly canned — for the thirsty construction workers.

Bill Johns and his executives had been quick to appreciate the importance of the developing Bougainville market. Before construction began, Johns and Bruce Flynn (who was appointed assistant general manager in 1971) visited Bougainville to assess the situation, and try to obtain a slice of the action for their product.

'In the initial stage we had massive battles with Bougainville Copper to get them to change their policy of total offshore supply,' Bill Johns recalled at a conference at Port Moresby in October, 1981. 'They had charter ships coming up from south with their raw materials — steel and so on, and even lolly water, beer, fruit, meat, vegetables, the lot. But they made a real mess of handling the incoming supplies, particularly the liquid refreshments. They found it impossible to keep track of where all that beer and lolly water went. So we moved in, and offered to take over the control of all the incoming drinks. We took control of each container, their man and our man would check the contents, and we would see that each lot of cartons got to the right outlets. For this we got a small fee per carton, but the big thing was we were able to get our draught beer in. And that's how we got a toe-hold in the new Bougainville market. Later on the mining company bowed to pressure from the village people and started to buy their fresh fruit and vegetables locally, and today the Bougainville operation is managed in Bougainville, not overseas.'

In 1970, South Pacific Brewery Ltd. formed a subsidiary company, Bougainville Beverages Pty. Ltd., with the express object of supplying the Bougainville district, and in particular the Panguna copper mine and the nearby administrative township of Arawa. Bougainville Beverages also manufactured, and distributed, a range of soft drinks. The company made an initial investment of $30,000 in Bougainville Beverages, and allotted 25 per cent of the called-up capital to two groups of Bougainville villagers, led by Severinas Ampeoi and Henry Moses. In the SPB annual report for 1970/71, chairman Jim Cromie noted that Bougainville Beverages Pty. Ltd. was formed 'upon the express understanding that this subsidiary, while in the early stages under Brewery control, would, as its ultimate aim, be entirely controlled by the indigenous people'.

Automotive keg filler, Lae Brewery.

For a number of years it had been obvious that the company would have to introduce canned beer, to counter the competition from the Australian brands that were so popular in Bougainville when the copper project got under way. In 1972 a canning line and associated equipment was installed at the Port Moresby brewery, at a cost of more than $250,000. Production of canned SP beer began in July, 1972. The Port Moresby brewery was now marketing seven different lines of packaged beer, plus draught. SP canned beer sold well, and helped to counter another looming threat: yet another local brewing company, which began to sell beer on 22 May, 1971.

At meeting No. 252 of the Land Board of PNG, held on 24 September, 1968, an application was lodged in the joint names of Raymond Lord, Geoffrey Martyn and Norman White for Allotments 40 to 46 inclusive, Section 52, Gordon's Estate, Port Moresby.

Giving evidence at the Land Board hearing, Norman White stated that a company would be formed to establish a brewery on the land. Directors would be himself, Lord, Martyn, W.N. Johns — a civil engineer and businessman — and C.R. Jackson, managing director of Papuan Airlines, owners of the new luxury Gateway Hotel, Port Moresby. Technical advisors to the brewing company would be Asahi Breweries Ltd. of Japan. Half a million dollars would be spent to establish the new brewery, and initial production was expected to be some 600,000 gallons per year.

This was the first definite indication that another brewery was to be established at Port Moresby, although rumours had been current for some time. Raymond Lord and Geoffrey Martyn were, of course, principals in the firm of Martyn, Lord and Fishwick, and Norman White had been involved in the original formation of South Pacific Brewery Ltd. As mentioned in the previous chapter, Lord had been appointed auditor of the company in 1960, a position he held until 1966, when he was replaced by A.C.Massam (who died in November of that year. The old-established firm of Peat Marwick Mitchell & Co then became the South Pacific auditors, a position they hold today).

The Land Board meeting (they were public meetings) was attended by

Open-cut copper mine at Panguna, Bougainville Island.

two staff members of South Pacific Brewery Ltd., Adrian Murphy and Raymond Priestley. Adrian Murphy, an accountant, joined the company in March, 1966, after experience with the big Sydney retailers, David Jones, and then with Farley and Lewers, of Ready Mixed Concrete fame. Ray Priestley joined in March, 1968, and became marketing manager. Their report to Bill Johns made it plain that a serious competitor would soon be active in the marketplace. A search in the office of the Registrar of Companies in October revealed that a company had, indeed, been formed, called 'Papua and New Guinea United Breweries Pty. Ltd.'. Bill Johns, looking at the evidence, wrote to Jim Cromie — who now lived in Melbourne — saying 'we conclude that the personnel involved have the ability, finance and technical assistance to complete the establishment of this project'.

The project was established, but it was to be even less successful than Guinea Brewery had been, and to have a much shorter independent life. The new brewing company was launched under the name, Territory United Brewery Ltd., with an authorised capital of $6 million. Issued capital amounted to $1,250,000, increased by $500,000 in 1971. Burns Philp (New Guinea) Ltd. was a heavy investor, and B.C.Goodsell, the BP general manager, became chairman of the board of directors, which included a number of prominent local businessmen: C.R.Jackson, A.J.S. Cotter, H.B.Ferguson and J.E.Roberts. The managing director was John Moray. South Pacific Brewery Ltd. was a small investor, with 500 shares.

The Administration granted Territory United Brewery Ltd. (TUB) a lease over the Gordon's Estate land. It was a choice site. The agreement with Asahi Breweries of Japan called for technological assistance in planning and building the new brewery and in its later operation, for which royalties would be charged. (Asahi Breweries in 1971 accepted 400,000 shares in lieu of royalties.) Two Asahi technicians inspected the Gordon's Estate land and pronounced it suitable for the compact, remote control-type brewery to be constructed. It was at first hoped that construction would be completed by September, 1969, with the beer being marketed late in November, but as so often happens with a new enterprise there were many early difficulties to be overcome, and the beer was not on sale until May, 1971.

Naturally enough, the management of South Pacific Brewery Ltd. kept as close an eye as possible on the operations of their rivals. The new TUB beer was launched with a considerable flourish, and virtually all clubs and hotels in Port Moresby stocked up with draught as well as bottled. Many outlets in other parts of PNG also took part in the launch. The new beer had a certain curiosity value and most drinkers tried it, but in just a few months sales of TUB beer had slowed, drastically. As South Pacific Brewery was itself to find in 1975, when it wasted much effort and cash on the ultimately unsuccessful launch of Anchor beer, brewed under licence from Archipelago Brewery (part of the Malayan Breweries group), it was hard to permanently wean beer drinkers from their favourite brew.

When assessing the probable effect of the release of TUB beer on the market, the South Pacific Brewery management had conceded that the company would lose a percentage of its natural growth, which had averaged approximately 18.5 per cent per annum over the preceding five years. Sales projections prepared by the marketing manager, Ray Priestley, predicted that Territory United Brewery would be selling 1,250,000 gallons per year by 1973/74, with SP sales estimated at 6,860,000. But only four months after the first TUB beer went on sale, it was obvious that it was not being accepted by consumers. All but three clubs in Port Moresby had stopped selling the draught, while still carrying the packaged beer. The Papua Hotel — owned by Burns Philp — pushed TUB vigorously, but the other BP pub, the Moresby, sold mostly SP. The Cecil Hotel in Lae had some success with TUB, but overall the new beer found scant favour throughout PNG. Unfortunately for Territory United Brewery, it hit the market at a time when the sale of imported beers was again increasing, and the production of SP beer was soaring. Territory United Brewery was soon in deep financial trouble.

The launch date of TUB beer was unfortunate for the company for another reason. On 23 August, 1971, a Commission of Inquiry into Alcoholic Drink had been set up, following intense debate in the House of Assembly[2], and the passing of a motion moved by the Member for Hagen, Pena Ou —

'That a Commission of Inquiry be set up to investigate all aspects of the liquor trade, and that this Commission make recommendations for any necessary alterations to the present liquor licencing laws deemed necessary, taking into account the oft-expressed concern of this House in the maintenance of law and order.'

As we have seen, the lifting of prohibition had been greeted with high enthusiasm by the PNG people, and at first there were few incidents of drunkenness, or rowdy behaviour. 'Never let it be said that the new drinkers can't hold their liquor,' said THE DRUM column, facetiously, in the *South Pacific Post* issue of 4 December, 1962. 'Seen in a pub on Saturday was a gigantic gentleman carrying three middies in either hand. And stuck down inside his laplap around his waist were a dozen small bottles. If that's not holding it, what is?'

As time went by, however, the incidence of drunkenness in the towns — where it was most visible — began to increase, and afforded little cause for amusement. The *Liquor (Special Provisions) Ordinance*, 1962, which had provided for a partial relaxation of prohibition, was replaced by the *Liquor*

Bottling hall, Lae Brewery.

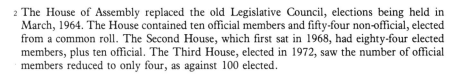

2 The House of Assembly replaced the old Legislative Council, elections being held in March, 1964. The House contained ten official members and fifty-four non-official, elected from a common roll. The Second House, which first sat in 1968, had eighty-four elected members, plus ten official. The Third House, elected in 1972, saw the number of official members reduced to only four, as against 100 elected.

(Licensing) Ordinance which came into force on 26 September, 1963. Papua New Guineans were henceforth allowed to consume alcoholic drinks under exactly the same conditions as Europeans. The 1963 ordinance established licencing districts within PNG, and a Liquor Licensing Commission, consisting of a full-time chairman, with two commissioners appointed for each district. Provision was also made for the appointment of a chief licensing inspector, and other inspectors and officers. Territorians generally were tickled when the post of chairman of the Liquor Licensing Commission went to senior magistrate Ralph Ormsby, famous for his physical size, his gargantuan appetite, and his capacity for strong drink. He was the only man ever provided with a seat at the New Guinea Bar at Usher's Hotel in Castlereagh Street, Sydney, the Mecca of Territorians on leave in Australia in the 1950s and 1960s, and where SP beer could be obtained.

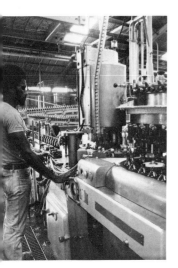

Bottling line, Lae Brewery.

The 1963 ordinance also ended the temporary ban on liquor advertising imposed by the 1962 law. South Pacific Brewery Ltd. had always advertised its products, using the outlets available — posters, hoardings, banners, giveaways, theatre slides, the local newspaper — but Rudolph Meier, the first manager, was not 'promotion minded' and in the early days relatively little was spent on advertising. A number of catchy slogans were developed, however, which became widely known through the company's newspaper advertisements.

The first of these SP slogans started to appear in November, 1953 — 'SP — It's Beer as Beer Should Taste!'. This was soon modified to 'It Tastes as Good Beer Should'. 'Drink South Pacific Lager — It's Good!' exhorted another popular slogan. In December, 1954, 'Whatever the Test — SP Lager's Best' joined the slogan stable. For some years these simple slogans were run in cheap ribbon advertisements across the bottom of the front and back pages of the *South Pacific Post*. Sometimes, for variety, 'Skip the Rest — Drink the Best — SP Lager' appeared.

The longest-lived of all the SP newspaper advertisements, featuring Susie (S) and Peter (P) cartoons of a girl and a youth facing each other, mouthing the virtues of the product, began to appear in 1958. Bill Johns was manager by this time, and the company's advertising had become more adventurous. In the first full-page SP newspaper advertisement, in August 1959, Susie the Housewife says brightly, 'I can entertain more now that SP is so progressive! Taxation[3] will certainly cut into the family budget, but thanks to SP it won't be too bad. I buy in cases, and save the empty bottles for return.' Peter, the Husband, agrees, and signs off with the immortal words, 'Be Specific, Say South Pacific!'. This slogan, used to the present day, was the winning entry in a Territory-wide competition held by the brewery, and was the invention of Bill McKelvey, an employee of the Commonwealth Department of Works.

[3] Income tax was introduced into PNG for the first time in 1959. It was bitterly resented by expatriates, and was the issue over which Jimmy James and the other two elected members of the Legislative Council, Dudley Jones and Ian Downs, resigned.

Bill McKelvey receiving his prize money for his winning entry in the SP slogan competition.

The temporary ban on liquor advertising was welcomed by both South Pacific and Guinea Breweries — the expense was becoming a sizeable item in the accounts of both companies — but the *South Pacific Post*, which derived welcome revenue from this source, was outraged. Hoardings, billboards and posters advertising SP beer were still freely in evidence, the newspaper pointed out. 'Into the Territory each week pour more than 5,900 Australian newspapers, each carrying considerable liquor advertising,' a reporter claimed.

The editor of the *Post* wrote a piece in the issue of 16 December, 1962, wherein he hinted, darkly, that there was a sinister purpose behind the advertising ban. 'The partial implementation of the liquor advertising ban is now shown to be no more than direct discrimination against the local newspaper', he wrote. 'The ban on newspaper advertising is inexorably enforced, but liquor hoardings, etc., by the hundred still continue to promote liquor in the most blatant way. The "Post" claims this is a militant, outrageous sanction against it for having kept alive the principle of pioneer journalism in the Territory, and for having exercised the right to criticise the Administration . . .'.

The advertising ban was eventually relaxed — before it was legally abolished by the 1963 ordinance — and guidelines were announced. South Pacific Brewery put into effect what was to be one of its most successful promotions ever — although results came in an altogether unexpected way.

The principal public transport service in Port Moresby in 1963 was a bus line, originally provided by the Administration, but now privately operated. The service covered all of Port Moresby and outlying districts, and the buses would obviously make prime mobile display units for SP advertisements. The company purchased the advertising rights, and contracted with signwriter Rudy Caesar to paint 'BE SPECIFIC SAY SOUTH PACIFIC' and enticing pictures of glasses of foaming SP ale across the backs of the vehicles.

The bus depot was located on the outskirts of the town, on land belonging to the London Missionary Society, not far from the Poreporena Church. One Sunday morning, the venerable LMS missionary, Rev. Percy Chatterton[4], who first came to Papua in 1924, emerged from the Church to face the rear ends of a row of buses, all strikingly adorned with beer glasses and the SP message.

Percy Chatterton was no bigot — he was a member of the 1962 Committee of Inquiry that recommended the swift relaxation of prohibition — but this seemed to him a bit much. The bus company duly received word from their landlords — unless the offending signs and pictures were removed, they would have to look for another depot. Urgent negotiations followed, and a compromise was reached. The pictures of glasses of beer were allowed to remain, but the slogan would be replaced by the simple

4 Now Sir Percy, and still living in Port Moresby, Chatterton was an elected member of the First and Second Houses of Asembly; a much loved and respected elder statesman of PNG.

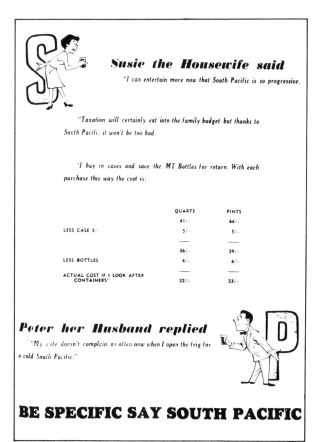

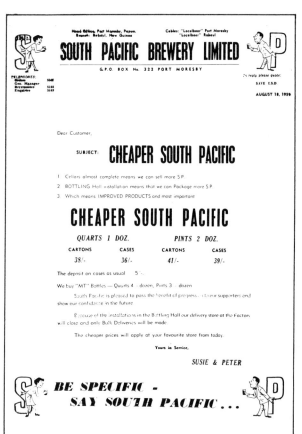

words, 'SAY NO!'.

Some young Papuan, bemused by this now clouded exhortation, wandered into a hotel bar a day or so later, and demanded a glass of No. The droll little story was printed in THE DRUM column of the *Post*, and was picked up by an international news service as an amusing 'filler'. Soon it was being published in newspapers throughout the world.

The 'Say No' story was chuckled over in towns and outstations all over the Territory, but it was becoming plain that the increasing abuse of alcohol by nationals was no joking matter. Hoteliers began to complain of the losses of hundreds upon hundreds of glasses. One riotous weekend in Port Moresby saw the arrest and conviction of seventy-one Papuans and one European, in what was described as the town's 'most drunken weekend ever'. A special sitting of the Court of Petty Sessions was required to cope with the situation.

With amazing rapidity, the overall position deteriorated. As early as December, 1962, the Director of the Administration's Department of Information and Extension Services, chaired a meeting attended by mission, government and welfare organisation representatives interested in promoting a Territory-wide temperance campaign. It was agreed that any campaign would have to be based on the right of the individual to make his own decision about drinking. Facts should be presented accurately and conservatively. The Administration would provide and disseminate factual information about alcohol and alcoholism, which would be available to all. The co-operation of sporting, social and religious organisations would be sought.

In January, 1963, the Queensland Temperance League announced that it was donating £7,500 to the anti-drink campaign over the next twelve months, with another £5,500 to follow. Two League officers would be specially trained in Brisbane and sent to PNG to assist the local effort. At the same time, training of national barmen began at a Port Moresby hotel, and in February Miss Joyce Hihera became the first Papuan girl to be employed as a barmaid!

In September, 1963, Paul Hasluck — almost at the end of his record term as Minister for Territories — felt compelled to make a statement in the Australian Parliament. 'Drinking is undoubtedly a problem in PNG following the removal of prohibition,' he said. 'The problem exists because people who previously were not accustomed to drink are now at complete liberty to drink.' The Administration was encouraging SEVA, the temperance society, and providing financial and other support, he told Parliament, and temperance education was being given in schools as a part of general science teaching.

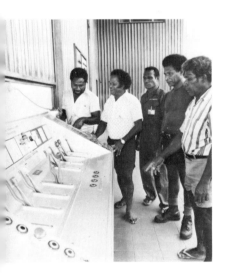

Control panel, Lae Brewery.

Unfortunately, the vaunted temperance campaign never really got off the ground, and consumption of alcohol by Papua New Guineans went on rising. The Liquor Licensing Commission came under attack in many quarters for the liberal way in which new licences were issued. The chairman, Ralph Ormsby, took the view that where there was a spontaneous demand in an area for a liquor outlet, it should generally be granted unless a good reason was advanced to the contrary.

In November, 1963, a petition signed by 1,595 people was presented to the Commission in support of an application by the Port Moresby Freezing Co. as agents for Moresby Hotel Ltd. for a tavern licence at Koki. The hearing that followed was the longest yet held by the Liquor Licensing Commission. The application was opposed by an extraordinary number of individuals and organisations. Predictably, SEVA, the Salvation Army and the Missions were solidly against a tavern at such a sensitive location as Koki, but so were the police, Native Affairs officers and the Department of Education, which planned to open two new schools in the vicinity. Koki was already a traffic hazard and a trouble spot, said a police spokesman. Even the Chief Licensing Inspector, Vern McNeil, opposed the granting of the application.

The Koki Tavern licence application was front-page news in Port Moresby for days. When the Commission decided unanimously to reject it, the *Post* headlines read, 'There Is No Tavern In The Town!'. There was at that time only one tavern in PNG, the Tortilla at Madang. Ormsby held that there was no objection to this type of outlet, if well sited, and many more tavern licences were issued over the following years.

By the end of 1964, there were 300 liquor licences in force throughout PNG. There were now twenty-two hotels. In addition to those previously mentioned, the following were in business: Hotel Boroko; Pine Lodge Hotel, Bulolo; Hotel Kavieng; Kundiawa Hotel; Kainantu Highlands Hotel; Minj Hotel; Mount Hagen Hotel; Wewak Hotel; England's Hotel, Angoram; Maprik Hotel; Daru Hotel; Hotel Kieta and the Lamington Hotel, Popondetta. Licenced social and sporting clubs were too numerous to list here — there were sixty-seven of them. Apart from thirteen restaurant licences, almost all the rest were storekeepers' licences.

'It's the Limit,' said the *South Pacific Post*. 'The time has come for a far tougher attitude by the Liquor Licensing Commission, particularly towards the granting of new storekeeper, tavern, club and restaurant licences... there is evidence enough in the streets of waste, drink-inspired brawls, a saddening fall in the otherwise high standard of social ethics inherent in Papua New Guinean citizens. The real tragedy is in the villages, and in the homes of better-class housing settlements such as Hohola. There, fear and want, directly created by liquor, has led to unhappiness in the last eighteen months which is unprecedented...'.

Ralph Ormsby, however, claimed that 300 liquor licences were 'not excessive', given PNG's population of over 2 million. New South Wales, with 4 million, had 4,542 licences. The Liquor Licensing Commission continued to respond to demands for additional outlets. Consumption of alcohol increased rapidly, year by year; reports of personal, family and social disruption throughout PNG multiplied; the liquor problem was discussed in homes, churches, council chambers, government circles, villages, in the newspapers and in the House of Assembly. The final result was the setting up of the 1971 Commission of Inquiry into Alcoholic Drink.

The Commission was chaired by a Supreme Court judge, Mr Justice Clarkson. The other Commissioners were all nationals; Dr Kahu Sugoho, Mrs Wasi Romney, Aloysius Noga and Phillip Paney. Their task was to investigate and report on alcoholic drink in PNG, and in particular on its effects on economic circumstances, health and social behaviour, including crime.

This was by far the most searching inquiry into alcohol and its effects yet carried out in PNG. The Committee sat in all districts between 19 August and 26 November, 1971, heard 386 witnesses and received 550 exhibits. Over 1,100 replies were received to a questionnaire sent by the Commission to community groups throughout PNG. Members of the Commission visited Fiji, the New Hebrides, the British Solomon Islands Protectorate, West Irian, Queensland and the Northern Territory.

The Report of the Commission, dated 22 December, 1971, made sobering reading. The general conclusion reached was that in PNG 'the consumption of alcohol is associated with a number of undesirable conditions

...many men spend an unduly high proportion of their cash income on drink...immoderate drinking by males has led to various forms of anti-social behaviour. In general terms, the possession and consumption of alcoholic drink have achieved a degree of importance at all levels of society which is quite unjustified in a developing country'.

The Commission found that in the seven years since prohibition was abolished, the consumption of beer had increased by three and a half times (from 1.6 million gallons to 5.5 million, 3.1 million of which was consumed by nationals), of spirits by three times and of wines by seven times. While the average wage earner in Australia spent about 4 per cent of his income on liquor, his Papua New Guinean counterpart spent around 20 per cent. In seven years the population had increased by one fifth, but there had been a ninefold increase in the incidence of crime, some of it alcohol-related.

The Commission was politely critical of the role of the Liquor Licensing Commission. 'The real criticism which emerged from the evidence is that the Liquor Licensing Commission has more often found that the public interest lay in granting a minority demand, than in ascertaining and accepting the wishes of the majority.' At 30 April, 1971, there were 644 licences in force, 459 of them storekeepers' licences, a number that outstripped the capacity of the police to supervise them. There were thirty-six publicans' licences, fifteen limited hotel and fourteen tavern licences in force. A total of 146 applications for licences of various kinds were outstanding.

The Committee made many recommendations, designed to reform the operations of the Liquor Licensing Commission, improve the location and supervision of licenced premises, upgrade the facilities provided for drinkers, modify trading hours and control liquor advertising. It recommended the establishment of a permanent body, financed from increased licence fees, to conduct research and liquor education programmes, and provide for specialist treatment as it became necessary.

One group of recommendations were of especial interest to South Pacific Brewery Ltd. Noting that the imposition of total or partial prohibition was against the wishes of responsible indigenous opinion and impracticable to enforce, the Committee recommended that the consumption of beer at the expense of other alcoholic drinks should be encouraged by increasing customs duties on spirits and fortified wines, creating 'beer only' licences for public bars and taverns and some clubs, fixing the alcoholic content of beer at 3.5 per cent by weight, and by the eventual prohibition of the sale of methylated spirits, still drunk by some Papua New Guineans.

The feelings of the Commission were clear and unambiguous; since Papua New Guineans were going to drink, the least harmful drink was beer, on the grounds that its alcohol content was far lower than spirits or wines.

Throughout the inquiry, Bill Johns and his senior executives provided at the request of the Commission a wide variety of information on the

GRASS ROOTS

MASSHKI...DISSHPELA
W-W-WISIKI I W-W-WINIM
..HIC... BLARY SSHPIRIT
HENITAIM......

TASOL EM
I BLARY
YUSLES LONG
LAITIM BLARY
TILILEMP IA...

Don't worry . . . . . this whisky beats bloody (methylated) spirit anytime.
But it's bloody useless for lighting the hurricane lamp here . . . . . .

The Health Department plans to restrict the sale of methylated spirits in trade stores.
The plan is a bid to cut down on the number of deaths caused by drinking the fluid.
Health Minister Mr Jaminan said he had instructed his department to prepare a submission proposing legislation against the sale of methylated spirit.

operations and financial results of South Pacific Brewery Ltd. Bruce Flynn prepared a chart showing the alcohol content by weight of all beers currently sold in PNG. South Pacific lager and a number of Continental beers still being imported (including Heineken and Amstel) contained 3.8 to 4 per cent alcohol. Territory United beer contained 4 per cent, as did Fosters Lager. Other Australian beers varied between 3.6 per cent (Resch's Pilsener) and 3.9 per cent (Carlton Draught, Melbourne Bitter and Castlemaine XXXX). There was no technical reason why SP lager could not be brewed to 3.5 per cent by weight. Forwarding this information to the Commission, Bill Johns made the point that a reduction in alcohol content to 3.5 per cent would hardly be noticeable. A reduction to 3 per cent however, would represent a drop of 21 to 25 per cent, a significant decrease.

The Committee did recognize the significant effects of the liquor industry upon the economy of PNG. It concluded that the liquor industry and its associated industries contributed some 12 per cent (between $8 and $9 million) of the internal revenue of PNG ($73,890,000 in 1970/71). Most of this came from locally brewed beer.

In coming to this conclusion, the Committee relied heavily upon a paper entitled 'Economic Analysis of the Consumption of Beer and Other Alcoholic Beverages in Papua New Guinea', prepared by W.R.Irlam, Principal Economist, Office of Programming and Co-ordination, using information drawn from many sources. Irlam attempted to assess the total share of national income provided by all industries connected with the production, transport, wholesaling and retailing of beer. Taking into account multiplier effects — stimulation of associated industries leading to increased demand for goods and services leading to increased employment, wages, company income etc — he calculated that the effect on national income would increase from $15,600,000 in 1970/71 to almost $28 million over the course of several years. Noting that employment in South Pacific and Territory United Breweries was slightly in excess of 500 — more than two thirds of them nationals — Irlam calculated that the total employment of persons connected with production, cartage and sale of alcoholic beverages amounted to some 4,600.

Irlam also drew attention to the high import replacement ratio of the PNG brewing industry — higher than any other local industry examined to that date. 'The brewing industry has already proved to be a catalyst to several other industries such as manufacture of glass bottles and fibreboard carton manufacture', he wrote. 'The breweries also provide by-products materials for use by other manufacturers...the industry has an impact upon the transport industry, and in Port Moresby efforts are being made to set up indigenous family transport units to transport beer from the factory gates to stores. Transport of brewery products by the coastal shipping industry is substantial. In 1970/71, 31,112 tons of products which included both full and empty bottles were shipped between various ports. This assisted to build up the intra-country freight load, and represented 18.2 per cent of the total coastal trade. Of significance to economic activity in the country as a whole is the fact that most of the retail and service activities concerned with making alcoholic beverages available to the general public are mostly fairly heavily labour-intensive.'

The 1971 Commission of Inquiry was undertaken at a particularly sensitive time in the history of PNG. The colonial era was almost at an end. In 1972 elections for the Third House of Assembly would be held. Michael Somare would emerge as Chief Minister — virtually the de facto Prime Minister — of PNG, head of a coalition government which would see the nation into self-government in 1973, and Independence in 1975.

After the elections, Somare and his Ministers would in fact be running the internal affairs of PNG, with little interference from Australia. It was going to be up to Papua New Guineans themselves to accept or reject the recommendations of the 1971 Commission of Inquiry.

Into the Seventies

The 1970s were to be momentous years for South Pacific Brewery Ltd. The company came into existence during the Australian colonial era, and for its first twenty years operated in a familiar and predictable business and political climate. The next ten years would bring fundamental changes. Business enterprises in PNG would have to learn to live with a completely new range of circumstances if they wanted to survive. An independent State of Papua New Guinea would impose its own restrictions and requirements on companies like South Pacific Brewery Ltd., born in colonial times, and still financed and controlled by non-citizens.

The company faced the new decade with confidence. It was a profitable concern, with an experienced management and a product in universal demand. Any brewing company is an obvious target for sectional criticism, particularly in a country like PNG, struggling to find its own feet, and with a liquor problem affecting a number of its people. Nevertheless, South Pacific entered the decade widely regarded as a reputable company, a good employer which paid its debts, abided strictly by the law of the land and demonstrated a responsibility towards the community from which it derived its profits.

South Pacific was fortunate to gain the services as director of Albert Lloyd Hurrell in December, 1969, after the sudden death of Mick Lloyd.

Lloyd Hurrell was a notable addition to the board. Government officer, soldier, farmer, politician and community leader, he was to receive the high award of C.M.G. in 1980 for his services to the community, and to the coffee industry. He was one of the few Australians to elect to take PNG citizenship after Independence.

Hurrell, from Wingham, NSW, came to PNG in 1939 as a cadet patrol officer in the old Department of District Services and Native Affairs. He enlisted in January, 1940, and went to war as one of the first contingent of the 2nd AIF to leave the Territory's shores. He served in the Middle East and New Guinea, joining ANGAU in 1944. His elder brother, Les, was killed in the New Guinea fighting. Lloyd Hurrell was himself severely wounded. He was awarded the Military Medal in 1942.

Returning to District Services after the war, Hurrell was posted as an Assistant District Officer to Salamaua, Morobe and Madang. In 1950 he was given the honour of establishing a new government station at Menyamya, in the wild Kukukuku country in the hinterland of the Morobe Goldfield. For two years he led a series of remarkable patrols through the partly-explored land of the Kukukuku, and then was transferred to Lae. He became Assistant District Officer, Wau Sub-District, in 1953, and the following year resigned to become a farmer and coffee planter in the Wau Valley. Lloyd Hurrell was for years a member of the Morobe District Advisory Council, an RSL office-holder, and was elected a member of the Legislative Council from 1958 to 1963. He served as chairman of the Coffee Marketing Board of PNG from 1965 to 1974.

Lloyd Hurrell, son Peter and Kukukuku friends at Menyamya, 1951.

Shortly after Hurrell's appointment as director, Max Lewis died. He was replaced on the board by J.D.H.Neill. Neill had been company secretary of Fraser and Neale and of Malayan Breweries, and upon the death of Max Lewis he took over as general manager of the group. An Englishman, born in Fiji, Neill had been a British colonial civil servant prior to taking up his business career, and was the holder of the M.B.E. He knew much of Chinese culture, and spoke fluent Cantonese. Neill had been closely associated with South Pacific Brewery Ltd. since the MBL takeover, and had a sound knowledge of the operations of the company.

Another businessman, an Australian, with extensive Asian experience joined the South Pacific board in March, 1973. He was W.W.Gawne, a Fraser and Neale executive who was captured by the Japanese in the fall of Singapore and spent the war in the notorious Changi prisoner-of-war camp. He resumed his career with Fraser and Neale after the war.

A major adjustment of the top management of the company took place in June, 1973, with the retirement of Bill Johns. John's ripe experience was not lost to South Pacific however, for he, too, was offered an appointment as director. Johns was replaced as general manager by Bruce Flynn. Ian Firth continued as company secretary. Adrian Murphy was now company financial controller, Ray Priestley remained marketing manager, and W.T. Barclay was appointed staff manager. Bruce Preston became head brewer.

Preston, a New Zealander, joined South Pacific Brewery in 1966. He was trained at New Zealand Breweries — now known as Lion Breweries — and later at Tooth & Co. in Sydney. He gained his degree in chemistry at Auckland University. He was sent to Lae as brewmaster soon after his appointment.

Lae had become too big an operation to be run by one man. On the arrival of Bruce Preston at Lae, Rudi Bertram took over the production side. Later, assistant brewer John Strong joined the Lae team. John Barnes, a young brewer who started work at the Port Moresby brewery in 1964 in the laboratory, became brewmaster in Lae after the promotion of Bruce Preston.

Bruce Preston, Technical Manager.

The departure of Bill Johns was a significant landmark in the history of South Pacific Brewery Ltd. Johns was a part of the old order. He had lived his life in the PNG of colonial times. Within months of his retirement, PNG attained self-government, and Independence was only two years away.

Bill Johns had been much more than a successful company manager. He had given freely of his time and talents to many causes, and had encouraged his executives to follow his example. In 1972 Johns was awarded the O.B.E. for community service. Under his management, South Pacific had supported a great variety of public activities, and contributed liberally to many charities. Johns himself had been chairman of the first Social Services Council. He chaired many fund-raising ventures for the St. Johns Ambulance Brigade, and was a foundation member and past president of the Port Moresby Rotary Club. A keen golfer, he was also a past president of the Port Moresby Golf Club. Johns was one of the original Associate Commissioners of the PNG Electricity Commission, and served on the board of the Investment Corporation.

Perhaps the most telling example of the esteem in which Bill Johns was held was his appointment to the position of executive director of the organising committee chaired by Sir Donald Cleland, charged with the responsibility by raising funds for the South Pacific Games Trust. The 1969 Games were a great event in modern PNG history. They did much to foster national pride, and a feeling of national identity among the people of a colony soon to become an independent State.

With the assistance of a subsidy from the Administration, Johns's committee eventually raised some K800,000, in cash and kind. This was sufficient to construct the main venue — the Sir Hubert Murray Arena —

and other facilities, and run the Games. South Pacific Brewery made a direct cash contribution of K10,000, and the tobacco company, Rothmans, was also a major contributor. The SP involvement was so extensive, however, that the value of its input was more like K100,000. Johns was executive director, Ian Firth was secretary and Adrian Murphy, treasurer. Company resources and facilities were freely co-opted, and company time used. Virtually everyone in the company head office, European and Papua New Guinean, found themselves working for the Trust. (Adrian Murphy remains a member of the Sir Hubert Murray Stadium Trust, formed after the Games to manage the day-to-day operation of the complex.)

Bruce Flynn, too, was heavily involved in the 1969 Games. Indeed, he had played a leading part in amateur sport since joining the company in 1955. It was largely through the influence of Bruce Flynn that South Pacific began to sponsor and assist sport in PNG, a story which will be told in later chapters of this book.

Flynn's personal credentials were impeccable. Before coming to PNG he had played professional football for Canterbury-Bankstown, and from 1955 to 1960 was captain-coach of the Magani rugby league football team. He became president of Magani, and senior vice-president of the Papuan Rugby League. During these years he also played baseball and basketball. When South Pacific took over Guinea Brewery (and at around the same time acquired a short-lived interest in South Pacific Beverages, Madang), Flynn became head brewer, and no longer had time to spare for active participation in football administration.

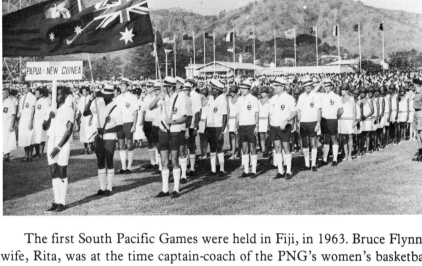

Above left *Sam Piniau (on right), attending the opening of Radio Mendi, 1978.*
Above right *Papua New Guinea's team at the 1969 South Pacific Games, Port Moresby.*

Below *John Natera.*

The first South Pacific Games were held in Fiji, in 1963. Bruce Flynn's wife, Rita, was at the time captain-coach of the PNG's women's basketball team, and together they attended the Games. On returning to PNG, Flynn became involved with the PNG Amateur Sports Federation in planning the 1969 Games. He represented the Federation on the South Pacific Games Council, and on the death of Don Barrett, acted as president of the Federation. He was replaced in this position in 1971 by a Papua New Guinean, Sam Piniau.

In 1973, the National Sports Council was formed by the then Minister for Sports and Youth, Moses Sasakila MHA. At the invitation of the Minister, Bruce Flynn became his representative on the Council, a position he holds to the present day.

In the tradition established by Bill Johns, Bruce Flynn was also active in general community affairs. He was an executive member of the Employers Federation of PNG, a foundation member of the Junior Chamber of Commerce and a member of the Port Moresby Rotary Club. He was to follow Bill Johns as a commissioner of ELCOM, the electricity commission.

Under Bruce Flynn, South Pacific Brewery Ltd. was to vastly expand the scope of its activities during the 1970s. Reviewing the decade shortly before his death, Bill Johns was generous in his praise of Flynn's leadership. 'In my time,' he said, 'it was a fairly small operation, and I was a stickler for maintaining the traditional image. With the arrival of Bruce in the chair, things suddenly escalated. Now it's a very big operation. Fortunately for the company, Bruce was able to bring management skills to it which I didn't possess. He was able to chart a new course for the company at just the right time.'

Bruce Flynn was assisted by a reorganisation of the capital structure of the company soon after he took over, a proposal that had been discussed by the board prior to Bill Johns's retirement. The reorganisation was chiefly planned and carried through by chairman Jim Cromie. On 20 September, 1973, South Pacific Holdings Ltd. was incorporated. The main operating company was still South Pacific Brewery Ltd., and the subsidiaries now were Guinea Brewery Ltd., Moresby Bottle Co. Ltd., Bougainville Beverages Pty. Ltd., and South Pacific Lager Distributors (Qld) Pty. Ltd., formed to distribute SP beer in Queensland. The nominal capital of South Pacific Holdings Ltd. was increased to $6 million.

One of the most significant consequences of the reorganisation was that local participation was now possible, and in 1974, 500,000 shares paid to forty cents were issued to the Public Officers Superannuation Board. They were fully paid up to one Kina[1] in 1974, and an outstanding Papua New Guinean, John Natera — the first of his race to graduate from a university, in 1965 — became a director, representing the Superannuation Board. Another 50,000 fully-paid one kina shares were allotted to the Defence Force (PNG) Retirement Benefits Board in 1975, bringing the percentage equity in Papua New Guinean hands to 9.25. This was to prove a wise move indeed.

Ian Firth[2] had in the meantime been obliged to resign as company secretary because of ill-health. Adrian Murphy took over temporarily, but the increasing complexity of operations of the South Pacific Holdings Group demanded the skills of a professional secretary. In May, 1975, Ron Corden was appointed to the position.

Corden, a lean, athletic man from Merseyside, had an interesting background. Born in 1937, he was a Fellow of the Institute of Chartered Secretaries and Administrators, London. Before coming to PNG, Corden had worked for the giant Unilever group, and then in the foreign department of the National Westminster Bank. He joined one of England's oldest shipping companies, Elder Dempster Lines, in 1964, handling aspects of the company's services to West African ports. He then became company secretary of an Anglo-French overseas bank in Lagos, Nigeria.

Ron Corden still had wanderlust, and he came to Australia. He joined a French bank in Sydney, but found the work too limiting. At this time the first government merchant bank in PNG was about to be formed. This was the PNG Investment Corporation, formed to buy shares in large companies owned by overseas interests, and sell them to Papua New Guinean individuals and organisations. Ron Corden was appointed company secretary of the Corporation. He came to Port Moresby in June, 1972. Three years later he joined South Pacific.

Corden took up his new career at a dramatic moment in the fortunes of South Pacific Brewery Ltd. On 12 May, 1975, a major fire broke out in the

1 On 19 April, 1975, PNG adopted her own currency. The main unit, the Kina, was made up of 100 Toea (both traditional terms). When the new currency was issued, it was exactly equivalent in value of Australian dollars and cents. In July, 1976, the first of what were to be many upward revaluations of PNG currency took place.
2 Firth died in July, 1982.

Lae Brewery. Flames raged for forty minutes through the bulk beer storage area and a cooling plant, before they were brought under control. Twelve-inch steel girders were twisted out of shape by the intensity of the heat. The brewery's own fire service was assisted by men and equipment from the huge Mobil fuel depot next door until the Lae fire brigade arrived.

What could have been a catastrophe was averted by the coolness and swift action of the firefighters. Although beer production was halted for several weeks, the stockpile of bottled and canned beer was sufficient to bridge the gap. The Port Moresby brewery increased production to the limit of capacity, and expert help was quickly available from the Heineken Group and Malayan breweries to repair the damage at Lae.

Fourteen months after the fire, the installation of eight huge new beer tanks, each with a capacity of 128,000 gallons, was completed at Lae at a cost of more than K1 million. Lined with stainless steel, they were built in Spain to a Heineken design, and were far more efficient than those destroyed in the blaze. The Lae brewmaster, John Barnes, was delighted with the new equipment. 'These tanks with their auxiliary equipment will allow us to make greater use of automatic controls,' he told a *Lae Nius* reporter, 'and will greatly improve working conditions for our employees in the fermenting and conditioning area.'

The long-term effects of the Lae brewery fire, therefore, were beneficial to the company. Insurance covered the damage, and development of the brewery was accelerated, helping the company to cope with the competition from the rival brewery. But at the time, the temporary loss of production capacity was an embarrassment, and not only so far as the domestic market was concerned (it was intended to supply all SP requirements for New Britain, New Ireland, the Highlands, Wewak, Madang, Manus and Popondetta from the expanded Lae Brewery). South Pacific Brewery Ltd. was also attempting to develop export markets.

As we have seen, SP beer had been sent to different overseas markets from early days. A favourite export target had always been Queensland, so close to PNG, physically and historically. In 1973, South Pacific Lager Distributors (Qld.) Pty. Ltd. was formed, to establish SP permanently in that State. Early efforts were directed at Cairns, the largest city in the Far North:

'Beer Invasion — Cheers!' ran an article in the Cairns *Focus News* in October, 1973. 'A large load of SP lager has arrived. Bob Stuart, export sales manager of SP Brewery, says it will sell at local prices...the shipment unloaded is a forerunner of large supplies on their way from the recently extended Lae brewery.'

On 9 April, 1974, the Mount Isa market was assaulted. 'Yesterday SP Brewery landed its green and brown bottles and cans in Mt Isa', the *North-West Star* told its readers. 'It is on sale at two hotels and most clubs. Bob Rennie, area sales manager for SP Lager Distributors (Qld.) says it is already on sale at Cairns and Townsville. It will sell at the same price as other beers in Mt Isa...'.

SP beer was available at this time in Sydney, at a number of outlets. It was sold at the Buena Vista Hotel at Mosman (patronised by officers of the PNG Administration attending the nearby Australian School of Pacific Administration); Cammeray Cellars; Jim Dorbis Liquor Supply; Claude Fay's Cellars, Beecroft; Boulevard Hotel, City; Hurstville Cellars; Hotel Manly; Liverpool Hotel; Mitchell and Co., Botany; Red Oak Cellars, Strathfield; Ermington Hotel, Ermington; Wholesalers Distributors, City; and Frangos Liquors Pty. Ltd., City. A sociologist could have plotted the enclaves of ex-Territorians and the favourite haunts of those down on leave from these outlets!

A great opportunity occurred in August, 1975. All breweries throughout Queensland went on strike, and thirsty drinkers went around for weeks with their tongues hanging out. But help was at hand! 'PNG is air-lifting beer to drought-stricken Cairns', the *Cairns Post* reported. 'SP Brewery has chartered an Electra to begin "mercy flights". Cairns has been dry for two weeks!'.

'Why stop at Electras?', asked THE DRUM column in the *Post-Courier*, Port Moresby[3]. 'This is an opportunity for PNG to get into a major export market. Why not a shuttle service of jets to Brisbane? Who knows — once Queenslanders get a taste of our brew, they mightn't want to switch back!'.

Sadly for South Pacific Brewery, however, Queenslanders did not acquire a lasting taste for SP beer. The brewery strike over, they went back to their favourite brews. (The same thing happened in 1979, when strikes again hit Queensland. Enormous quantities of SP were imported to save Queensland beer drinkers from dying of thirst, but once normal supplies were restored, the sales of SP dropped right off). In 1977, the South Pacific board took a reluctant decision to sell SP Lager Distributors (Qld.). It was no longer a profitable undertaking.

---

[3] The *Papua-New Guinea Post-Courier* first appeared on 30 June, 1968. It combined the old *South Pacific Post* with the *New Guinea Times-Courier*, which had been published in Lae.

10

`Operation Moderation`

The 1971 Commission of Inquiry into Alcoholic Drink had focussed the attention of the nation on what was clearly a problem of serious proportions, but action to implement the recommendations in the Report was slow to follow. The government failed to mount a liquor education programme. Exciting constitutional changes were taking place in PNG, and the liquor problem was obscured by other matters. However, in 1973 three Bills were passed in the House of Assembly, designed to give effect to certain of the Commission's recommendations. These were the *Liquor (Licensing) Bill*, the *Liquor (Miscellaneous Provisions) Bill*, and the *Motor Traffic Amendments Bill*. The first two Bills became law in January, 1974.

The new liquor laws introduced some important changes. Trading hours were reduced and two new classes of licence — dealers and bottle shop — were created. New licences and licence renewals would generally be issued on the condition that only beer, and not spirits, could be served in public bars (subject to exceptions granted by the Liquor Licensing Commission). Section 5 of the *Liquor (Miscellaneous Provisions) Ordinance* prohibited the advertising of all liquor *except* beer, ale, porter, stout and perry other than on licenced premises, and beer advertising, too, could be prohibited by the High Commissioner by notice in the *Government Gazette*.

The new legislation required the Liquor Licensing Commission to determine the wishes of the people before granting new licences in any area. Bodies known as Local Advisory Committees were set up, to ascertain the people's views for the Commission.

The appointment of Ralph Ormsby as chairman of the Liquor Licensing Commission had terminated on 25 September, 1971. He was replaced by V.B.McNeil, previously chief licensing inspector. Vern McNeil was a most capable chief of the Commission, during a very difficult time of rapid change.[1] When McNeil left PNG, a young national magistrate, Phillip

---

[1] As District Commissioner of the Eastern Highlands, the author was one of the two Liquor Commissioners for the district, and attended hearings over a number of years with Ralph Ormsby and Vern McNeil.

Early in 1975, a remarkable young Highlander was appointed Chief Liquor Licensing Commissioner. John Nilkare, from a village near Omkolai in the Chimbu District, received his early education in the Catholic Mission school system, and in 1965 attended the Administration High School at West Goroka. He graduated in 1968, and joined the Department of District Administration as a cadet patrol officer. At this time far-reaching changes in the courts system of PNG were under way, and bright young nationals were being sought for training as Local Court magistrates. John Nilkare became a magistrate. He served in a number of locations in the Highlands — Kundiawa, Kerowagi, Chuave — and in 1972 was transferred to Wau, in the Morobe District.

Wau was an important posting for John Nilkare. While at Wau he won a Churchill Trust scholarship, to study village courts and courts generally in Kenya, Tanzania and the Solomon Islands. Years later, Nilkare was one of those responsible for the introduction of village courts, and women magistrates, to PNG.

It was during his service at Wau that John Nilkare became interested in politics, like so many other educated Papua New Guineans at this time. He joined the Pangu Party, and campaigned actively in the 1972 House of Assembly elections for Boyamo Sali, who became a Minister in the Somare Coalition Government. He formed close links with Michael Somare and the leaders of the Pangu Party.

August 1982 saw John Nilkare achieving a life-long ambition when he became a Minister in the second Somare Government, responsible for the Decentralisation portfolio.

In 1974, Nilkare studied law part-time at the University of Papua New Guinea and topped his class. He was posted to Lae, where John Pritchard was senior magistrate. Nilkare was preparing to return to UPNG to resume his law studies when he received a message, saying that the grand old man of PNG politics, John Guise[2], wanted to see him.

John Nilkare.

'It was 17 January, 1975,' John Nilkare told the author in January, 1982. 'John Guise was Minister for the Interior then. I hadn't met him before. He said to me, "I want you to be Chief Licensing Commissioner. I have heard a lot about you". This was really great, you know? Magistrates were class six officers then, the Chief Licensing Commissioner was class eleven! Much more responsibility, and a much bigger salary. And I was only a young bloke. John Pritchard said to me, "No, John! You must go back to the university and get your law degree, and you'll become a Judge". But I took the Chief Licensing Commissioner job.'

As Chief of the Licensing Commission, John Nilkare naturally had official contacts with the management of South Pacific Brewery Ltd. In 1976, his involvement intensified with the launching of a project that was given the title of 'Operation Moderation'.

2 Guise was knighted on becoming Governor-General of PNG, on 16 September, 1975.

GRASS ROOTS

H... MISTA NBC... INAP BAI YU
PUTIM ADVETISMEN BILONG
MIPELA TU?...

EM NAU!!

A DAY WITHOUT BEER

IS A DAY WITHOUT FEAR

WHY DON'T WE JUST BAN BEER

Hey... Mr. N.B.C. (National Broadcasting Commission) can you put our advertisement on, too?
— There!

Women's representatives who met in Port Moresby yesterday will urge the Minister for Youth and Family Services, Mr Zurenuoc, to oppose moves to re-introduce beer advertising.

Operation Moderation was entirely a South Pacific Brewery initiative. It was an ambitious programme of social education, designed to encourage Papua New Guineans to drink sensibly, its genesis a continuing abuse of alcohol which was bringing down bitter criticism upon the liquor industry in PNG.

Year by year, Papua New Guineans were increasing their consumption of alcohol. By 1975/76, it was estimated that annual spending had reached K40 million. The newspapers were crammed with stories of drunken brawls, drink-driving offences — some involving Parliamentarians and community leaders — assaults on women, beer riots and black markets. Licenced traders were calling for protection for their staffs from drunken customers.

In the Highlands, gangs of 'rascals' began to raid the trucks hauling beer from Lae, stealthily boarding the labouring vehicles as they crawled up steep grades, slashing open the tarpaulins covering the loads and throwing down the cartons of beer to their accomplices. Police were almost powerless to stop these fleet-footed gangs. One Goroka contractor, A.A. Thick, lost thousands of dollars worth of beer and bagged rice in a few days, and his was a common experience. Jack Thick was a tough customer, the first man to undertake the regular road haulage of SP beer into the Highlands, a man who thought nothing of man-handling massive quantities of beer across landslides and who always got his cargo through. When he was moved to complain of the actions of the 'rascals', it was a measure of the seriousness of the situation. In Port Moresby, the City Council formed a 'Law and Order Committee' to devise ways of controlling the depradations of teen-aged gangs in the capital.

In an effort to stem the tide, the government banned the sale of liquor on Christmas Day, New Year's Day, during Easter and finally on all public holidays. During 1974 and 1975 the women of PNG began to voice their anger at the drinking habits of their men, calling for liquor bans, fewer liquor outlets and higher licence fees. The first National Convention of Women passed a series of recommendations to Cabinet, all aimed at firmer liquor control, criticising the evil effects of spirits consumption and calling for beer to be the sole alcoholic drink sold in PNG. This criticism by women was something new in PNG, where women in general were not encouraged to openly contradict the opinions of men.

There were other significant developments in 1975. John Nilkare asked local government authorities to take a bigger role in recommending who should get liquor licences. In July, the Kainantu Local Government Council was granted a liquor licence. A new hotel for Lorengau was announced in November, the shareholders in the venture the Manus Area Authority, the Manus Co-operative Society and a private company. Other local authorities were soon to become involved in liquor trading. Some were anti-liquor. The Port Moresby Council moved to ban Sunday liquor trading, and the Goroka Council demanded a completely 'dry' Independence Day — 16 September. A private member's bill was passed in Parliament in October, calling for a ban on liquor sales on government paydays. This became law in Port Moresby in December, and what became known as 'Thirsty Thursday' was eventually extended to other major centres. The government increased the excise duty on beer and spirits in the 1975 Budget. Vigorous beer black markets started to appear, fuelled by the payday bans. They accounted for the illegal sale of enormous quantities of beer at high prices. As soon as one black market was broken up by the police, others appeared.

Liquor was only one component — although highly visible — in the deterioration of law and order in PNG that had begun to manifest itself in the major towns and in the Highlands during the 1960s, and which accelerated after Independence. Why this situation occurred is beyond the scope of this book. Very simply put, it resulted from a premature dismemberment of the system of law and order that had served the country during most of the colonial era before an adequate substitute was developed. This dismemberment was done by Australia. Traditional forms of authority, irreparably weakened by the impact of Western civilisation, were no longer available. Tribal fighting began in parts of the Highlands where peace had reigned for twenty years under the old order. So concerned was the Administration that in 1972 Phillip Paney was appointed Chairman of the Highlands Violence Study Group, following the savage slaughter of two outstanding national public servants — Dr Luke Rovin and Peter Moini — by tribesmen near Goroka. Paney's Group submitted a long series of recommendations to the government on measures to control the Highlands situation. Liquor abuse was not then considered to be a dominating factor in the decline of law and order in the Highlands, although alcohol undoubtedly played a major role in traffic fatalities. Traffic accidents throughout PNG killed and mutilated far more people than did tribal fighting.

The rising tide of criticism of the liquor industry was intensified by the increasing use of advertising by the brewers. After the passing of the *Liquor (Miscellaneous Provisions) Act*[3] the off-premises advertising of wines and spirits was no longer legal, but no restrictions were placed on beer advertising. Competition for the beer market, by far the most important segment of the liquor industry (by 1975/76, wine consumption in PNG had fallen by 33 per cent and of spirits by 36 per cent), was fierce, and naturally the brewing companies and beer importers employed advertising in their fight for sales. South Pacific Brewery was still the market leader, with 92.4 per cent of the market in June, 1975. This market share declined in the following quarter, to 87.1 per cent principally because of aggressive activity by the rival brewery in Port Moresby, now owned by San Miguel and Swan Holdings Limited (known, jocularly, as 'SMASH').

[3] After Independence, the ordinances passed by the Australian Administration, and all new laws, were called 'Acts'.

GRASSROOTS

...ER...YU SINDAUN MALOLO MAI DALIN.. MI YET MI INAP HELPIM YU LONG GO KISIM WARA LONG CREEK..

FIRST TIME IN BLARY 25 YEARS!

HURRY   HURRY

Er ... you sit down and relax my darling ... I'll help you by getting the water from the creek ....

The cartons were on a Pagini transport truck which missed the narrow bridge at Kefamo and flew through the air. crashing into the rocky river-bed at about 2am.

Territory United Brewery Ltd. had had a short life. Initial under-capitalisation proved to be a stumbling-block that could not be surmounted, and on 19 August, 1972, Bert Goodsell, the TUB chairman, wrote to shareholders, advising them of the 'very serious financial situation' of the company. A consolidated nett loss of almost $800,000 had been made over the period 1/7/70 to 31/5/72. Secured and unsecured creditors amounted to more than $900,000. Brewing had ceased in March, 1972. The company was completely without funds. Goodsell recommended TUB shareholders to accept a takeover offer made by the San Miguel Corporation and the Australian company, Swan Brewery Co. Ltd. of Perth. Urgent action was required if TUB were to be saved from the ignominy of liquidation.

The offer — of one fully paid share of fifty cents each for every three TUB fifty-cent shares — was accepted, the takeover being completed on 21 February, 1973. Acquisition of Territory United Brewery had been considered by the South Pacific board as early as October, 1971, to keep the rival brewery from falling into the hands of foreign interests, but no action followed. It would, in any case, have been difficult for South Pacific to win any takeover battle with the likes of San Miguel and Swan.

The giant San Miguel Corporation began as a small brewery in Manila in 1890, and by the 1970s was one of the world's major brewing complexes. San Miguel operated three breweries in the Philippines, three in Spain, one in Hong Kong and one in Guam. It had large interests in a whole range of industries apart from beer. The Corporation had enormous financial strength, and was by any estimation a formidable adversary.

The Swan Brewery Group, while not in the same league as San Miguel, was still much bigger than South Pacific. Swan beer was sold in some sixty countries, 1,000 gallons per day being exported from Western Australia's main port of Fremantle. The Group also operated thirty hotels, and a chain of liquor stores among other interests.

San Miguel and Swan Holdings Ltd. was established with an authorised capital of $4.5 million. The chairman of directors was Andres Soriano Jr, president of the San Miguel Corporation, and included on the board were Bert Goodsell and C.R.Jackson. A Swan executive, Barry Walsh, was brought to Port Moresby as the first general manager of what came to be known as 'San Mig' to PNG beer drinkers. (The operating company was actually called Papua New Guinea Brewery Pty. Ltd.)

The task facing the new company was far from easy, despite the financial muscle behind it. It had taken over an organisation which was in dire financial and operating straits, and which had produced a beer that had been rejected by most consumers. A tremendous effort would be required to put matters right, produce new beers and persuade the drinkers of PNG to try and accept them. San Mig's obvious target was the market leader, South Pacific Brewery, and battle was swiftly joined; a trade war that has persisted, with periods of relative calm, to the present day.

San Mig and Swan launched their new brews with a four page colour

Colin Bice, Port Moresby's resident professional golfer is sponsored by SP Brewery. He conducts regular golf clinics for Papua New Guinean children.

Jerry Lamasisi (left) and Nicholas Toram are members of the martial arts club Tae Kwon Do, one of the many sports clubs assisted financially by the SP Brewery.

supplement in the *Post-Courier* on 10 May, 1973. Four new beers were offered, in stubbies with new, and convenient, rip-top caps as well as draught. They were San Miguel Export Beer, San Miguel Pilsener, Swan Draught and Swan Lager. They made an immediate impression on the market. The rip-top cap was especially popular, and was eventually adopted by South Pacific Brewery.

The rival breweries stepped up their advertising as the battle for the beer-drinkers' dollars escalated. The SP advertising budget was increased from $143,000 in 1969/70 to almost $400,000 in 1974/75. San Mig and Swan poured a lot of money into expensive colour spreads in the newspapers and on posters. The Swan labels featured a black swan, and San Mig's the company shield. 'Shortly, there'll be more Swans and Shields in PNG than palm trees!', one advertisement boasted. By the end of 1976 the new beers had captured almost 15 per cent of the PNG market.

As mentioned earlier, the increasing use of advertising attracted severe criticism from many quarters. Few critics were prepared to allow the breweries any virtues. Another point of view was put in a letter published in the *Lae Nius* in August, 1975, written by Glenn B. Watterson, National President, Apex Clubs of PNG:-

'The breweries are under attack from politicians and other groups on the size of their advertising budgets. Anyone associated with service or sporting bodies knows that a large proportion of these budgets is spent in the direct subsidisation of these bodies, and not in straight-out "flogging of beer"...without this we would not be able to function financially and carry out work in the community...it is not only a headache that emits occasionally from the notorious bottle, but in many cases financial help for embattled voluntary organisations fighting increased costs on shoe-string budgets, trying to improve the community they live and work in.'

Both South Pacific Brewery and San Mig-Swan did indeed spend heavily on sports sponsorship and on assistance to service clubs and other bodies. In the case of South Pacific, this form of advertising began in the 1950s and increased during later years. Of course the company gained from this policy, but so did a wide range of organisations whose successful operation would have been imperilled without SP money.

Very early in its existence, South Pacific began to assist Red Cross activities in Port Moresby, and later in other centres. It supported the various agricultural shows that have become a feature of life in many PNG towns, the first of which began, appropriately enough, in Wau, in 1950. (The first of the world-famous Highland Shows was held at Goroka, in 1956.) Golf was one of the first sports sponsored in a large way by the company. Events such as the 'South Pacific 500' for professional golfers, held in June, 1963, attracted entries from many countries. By the early 1970s South Pacific Brewery Ltd. was contributing to the administration and operation of many sports, from the major games — cricket, and the various football codes — to such minority pastimes as squash, game fishing, archery, pistol shooting, yacht racing and water skiing.

For years South Pacific sponsored a 'Social and Sporting Guide' in the local newspapers. At no cost to themselves, social and sporting bodies were able to advertise details of fixtures and events. The 'Guide' appearing in the *Post-Courier* in the issue for 3 October, 1974, was typical, and indicates the vast range of activities in the towns of PNG at that time, most of which received support of one kind or another from South Pacific. Listed in this 'Guide' were notices from the following bodies:-

SP Hawks Davai Thomas is the tireless tough 2nd Rower who is an 80-minute player. He has represented Southern Zone on many occasions and has an international match to his credit. SP Hawks are sponsored by SP Brewery.

Mike Brady in Port Moresby. He wrote the Commonwealth Games Team song for the PNG team.

Hash House Harriers — Port Moresby Run No. 43
Children's Fashion Parade
Moresby Amateur Swimming Club
Granville Speedway
Port Moresby Baseball Association
Youth Hostels Association
Port Moresby Soccer Association
Port Moresby Touch Football Association
Port Moresby Judo and Self Defence Classes
1974 SP Fishing Classic
Boroko Amateur Swimming Club
YMCA Swimming Carnival
Port Moresby Squash Association
Port Moresby Tennis Club
Early Birds Social Golf Club
Shell 100 Water Ski Marathon
Port Moresby Golf Club
Port Moresby Table Tennis Association
Polocrosse Club
Papuan Turf and Equestrian Association
Air Niugini Ball Committee, Wewak
Lady Lions Club of Wewak
Lae Army Sailing Championships
Koitaki Country Club
Goroka Gumi Ball Committee
Port Moresby Pistol Club
Small Bore Rifle Club
National Sports Events news: Lae, Rabaul, Madang, Wewak, Kavieng, Kundiawa, Kieta, Goroka (covering darts, pistol shooting, cricket, golf, basketball, sailing, korfball, soccer, bowls)

In addition to the above, the 'Guide' published on 31 October, 1975, printed notices from:-

Port Moresby Theatre Group
Port Moresby Game Fishing Club
Port Moresby Full Bore Rifle Club
Ela Motors Rugby League Club

Peter Hayworth, golf champion, proceeding on leave with his golf clubs etc.

Port Moresby Underwater Club and Sub-Aqua Club
Kone Tigers
Koboni Football Club
Port Moresby Darts Association
Port Moresby Stamp Club
Boroko CWA
Graphic Arts Association of PNG
Germania Club
Kavieng Baseball Association
Mt Hagen Gun Club
Madang Baseball Club
Lae Golf, Cricket, Squash, Sailing and Clay Target Shooting Clubs.

This kind of support for social and sporting organisations might perhaps be expected of a major brewing company, but the thought, time, effort and cash that went into the 'Operation Moderation' project referred to earlier, was surely unusual. For the Brewery was deliberately and carefully planning to educate its principal customers, the people of PNG, to limit their consumption of its product.

Operation Moderation did not spring into being overnight. Concerned at the mounting criticism of the brewing industry, Jim Cromie and his board in November, 1973, commissioned the first of a number of research studies by Spectrum International Marketing Services Ltd. into the beer market, and the behaviour and attitudes of Papua New Guineans towards

Presentation by Bruce Flynn of the SP Export Lager Cup, to the President of the Bougainville Rugby League, Barry Middlemiss.

beer. The principal recommendation emerging from these studies was for South Pacific Brewery Ltd. to initiate a large-scale educational programme. Spectrum's research had led to three primary conclusions:-

    (a) most people in PNG had not been sufficiently well educated in the use of alcohol; how to recognise varying levels of intoxication, and how to control them;

    (b) very few people were motivated to stop drinking once they had started, and

    (c) people in PNG generally drank to get drunk.

These conclusions pointed to one overriding need — that of teaching the drinker how to drink. PNG had no history of alcohol use. Alcohol — or, indeed, narcotic drugs of any kind — had no place in her traditional cultures[4]. Access to alcohol had come overnight, historically speaking, and before the people had had the opportunity of learning how to cope with it. As the market leader, and a company that had profited handsomely from alcohol, South Pacific had a responsibility to the PNG people to educate them.

In June, 1974, the SP board approved a substantial budget for the development of a suitable education programme. This work was to extend over a period of almost two years, and involved consultations with the PNG government, church groups, licensees, sociologists, anthropologists, communications consultants and individuals. A number of concepts were worked up by the company's advertising agency, Magnus Nankervis and Curl, before final agreement on a format was reached.

It was to be expected that it would be no easy matter to convince the government and individual Ministers of the urgent need for an education programme, and of the sincerity of the motives of South Pacific Brewery Ltd. There was a great deal of scepticism in many other quarters. Why should a brewing company undertake such a programme? Surely it was a job for an impartial body, preferably the government? Was it merely a political white-wash, to improve the public and political image of South Pacific Brewery and so in the end lead to increased beer sales? Particularly hard to convince was the redoubtable Pita Lus[5], Minister for Corrective Institutions and Liquor Licensing, himself a teetotaller with strong opinions on the liquor question.

It was largely through the influence of John Nilkare, Chief Licensing Commissioner, that the Minister was won over and Cabinet approval obtained for Operation Moderation. Nilkare was certain from early talks that he had had with Bruce Flynn and other SP executives that the company was genuinely concerned about PNG and the welfare of its people, and not just worried about its position in a country on the verge of Independence.

4 This does not exclude the minor narcotics such as betel nut, *kava* and etc.
5 Now Sir Pita

Certainly South Pacific Brewery Ltd. had a large stake in PNG, which it wanted to preserve. In mid-1975 the company employed 633 people, 92.4 per cent of them nationals. It provided housing for 210 of its national employees, and was by this time training them in increasing numbers to take over more responsible positions in the company. It was a major contributor to the economy of PNG. Thus, in the financial year 1975/76, the company made a nett profit of K1,318,231, and paid the government K12.5 million in excise duty and taxes. Operation Moderation could perhaps be described as a policy of enlightened self-interest, but it surely was an unusual programme for a brewing company to initiate, fund and carry through. And without advertising advantage. No mention of the SP involvement would be made in the posters, films and displays that would carry the Operation Moderation message throughout PNG.

An 'Operation Moderation Co-ordinating Committee' was formed, under the chairmanship of John Nilkare. The deputy chairman was Luke Sela, deputy director of the government's Office of Information. The Committee included representatives from the Education, Health and Welfare departments, local government, social welfare groups and the breweries. The Churches were invited to participate but declined, although promising their moral support.

Operation Moderation was officially launched on 24 March, 1976. An

amount of K150,000 was provided by South Pacific to cover the first year's activities, with future budgets to be decided later, for Operation Moderation was envisaged as a five-year programme, at least. Nobody was expecting quick miracles. The theme of the operation was: BE SMART-DON'T DRINK TOO MUCH. This message was mainly carried in a series of large advertisements in English, Pidgin and Motu in all newspapers and journals; over the radio; and in two colour films and a number of slides, eventually screened in more than thirty picture theatres and clubs throughout PNG. A variety of games and competitions, carrying cash prizes, were also devised.

Operation Moderation was applauded in an editorial in the *Post-Courier*:-

'Moderation means not given to extremes, keeping within reasonable bounds, measured, temperate, sober . . . when it comes to drinking alcohol, only a fool would disagree with the properness of moderation . . . excessive drinking has now become an alarming social problem. It's for this reason that South Pacific Brewery Ltd. is financing the campaign called "Operation Moderation".

'The Brewery is to be complimented. No matter what the cynics say this approach is proper, responsible and in the public and brewery's interest. As announced by the Minister for Corrective Institutions and Liquor Licensing, Mr Lus, the campaign — the first of its kind in the world

— is designed to eliminate the social problems of excessive drinking... sensibly, it does not advocate a halt to drinking. The American experiment with prohibition proved the folly of that approach. Drinking is here to stay, like it or not. It's how we drink, and how much, that matters. The campaign deserves whole-hearted public support.'

During 1976, Operation Moderation posters and advertisements were familiar sights all over PNG. Each featured cartoon characters in a variety of situations illustrating the evil effects of immoderate drinking on the individual and his family. The first to be used showed a sad-faced man turning out his empty pockets, with a caption ramming home the message, 'Too much beer can make you poor. Be smart! Don't drink too much'. Others were variations on this general theme. 'Too much beer can get you into trouble'; 'Too much beer can make you unhappy'; 'The money I save drinking less beer helps look after my family'; 'The money I save drinking less beer helps pay for my house'; 'The money I save drinking less beer helps to pay for my bike'.

None of the posters — all professionally drawn and designed — carried any SP advertising of any kind. The initials OM, followed by a very discreet 'Operation Moderation. An educational programme prepared in the interests of the people of Papua New Guinea', was the only identification.

San Miguel-Swan announced in February, 1976, that they, too, would launch a 'Drinking in Moderation' campaign, with a budget of around K50,000. San Mig representatives attended early meetings of the Operation Moderation Co-ordinating Commmittee, and their efforts were intended to complement that of South Pacific Brewery. The then general manager of San Mig-Swan, Jim Williams, explained to the meeting held on 10 March that the total assets of his company in PNG were valued at over K3 million whereas accumulated losses amounted to K2.5 million, which limited the effort that could be made. San Mig in fact played a limited part in Operation Moderation.

Sadly, Operation Moderation was halted long before any demonstrable results were achieved. Even as the programme was under way the consumption of beer was increasing, and the overall effects of alcohol abuse becoming more obvious. John Nilkare himself came under heavy attack from women leaders of PNG for his approval of licenced village clubs on the Gazelle, a move which he felt would encourage the men to drink moderately at home rather than in the hotels in the towns. In February, 1977, Nilkare resigned his position as Chief Licensing Commissoner to contest the Chimbu Regional seat in the national elections. (He was narrowly defeated by Iambakey Okuk, who became deputy leader of the Chan Coalition Government.)

On 27 January, 1977, the Liquor Licensing Minister, Pita Lus, announced that the National Executive Council had decided to ban the off-premises advertising of beer, as was already the case with wines and spirits. The breweries were given one month to remove advertising in theatres, newspapers and on signs. Brewery-owned vehicles would be permitted only to carry their respective company's corporate symbols. 'The Cabinet believes that it is a contradiction to allow advertising aimed at promoting drinking, while simultaneously taking various Government action to decrease drinking,' the Minister said.

In June, 1977, Lus withdrew his support of Operation Moderation, forcing the abandonment of the programme. John Nilkare speaking as a private citizen said in an interview published in the *Post-Courier* on 10 June that he was 'ashamed' of the position adopted by Pita Lus. 'It was too soon to judge whether the programme has had the right effect on the community,' Nilkare said. 'It has only been running for twelve months. Mr Lus should have consulted the OM Co-ordinating Committee before banning the programme. At the beginning, he was all in favour of having a non-government body telling Papua New Guineans to drink in moderation.'

So Operation Moderation failed, but not through any fault of commission or omission by South Pacific Brewery Ltd. The total amount expended on the programme by the company from the beginning in November, 1973, was close to K250,000.

In 1980, the Government toyed with the re-introduction of an OM-type programme as alcohol abuse continued, but nothing came of it. To date, Operation Moderation is the only national liquor education programme that has been attempted in Papua New Guinea.

'Bird Man' Bill Flewellyn flies in for a perfect landing at the Highlands Show.

Jumbo performing tricks.

11

Of Jumbos and Birdmen

The National Executive Council's decision of February, 1977, to ban the advertising of beer except on licensed premises created practical problems for the breweries. A strict interpretation of Section 5 of the *Liquor (Miscellaneous Provisions) Act 1973* would have been difficult to insist upon. In PNG, company indentification was required by law in certain instances — there were various Customs and Excise requirements with regard to labelling and packaging of products; transport had to be clearly marked with the owners name, and so on — and the government recognized this. Following discussions between the two breweries and the government, a set of guidelines was agreed upon. A notice in the *Government Gazette* on 14 March, 1977, permitted the breweries to display 'business names, devices, signs or symbols' in use to that date, provided that they were not used 'in a manner which is intended, or likely to promote, the sale or disposal of liquor, or to increase the purchase, consumption or use of liquor'.

Following the national elections in June/July, 1977, Mrs Nahau Rooney became Minister for Corrective Institutions and Liquor Licensing. She was zealous in the performance of her duties, and was quick to pull the breweries into line if she considered the spirit, let alone the letter, of the law was being flouted. SP marketing men had to be careful indeed not to wound the sensibilities of the Minister. The rules of the game were now being laid down by the independent State of Papua New Guinea, and had to be obeyed. No longer was it possible to mount the kind of spectacular advertising stunt that had in the past boosted the sales of SP beer, and at the same time assisted some worthy cause; stunts like the coming of Jumbo the Elephant, and the feats of the Birdman, Bill Flewellyn.

The sport of hang-gliding was in its infancy in the early 1970s. A handful of brave men were pioneering the sport, mainly in America and Europe, and it was yet to catch on in Australia. No hang-glider had flown in PNG.

As mentioned previously, South Pacific Brewery Ltd. had supported the various Agricultural Shows in PNG from the early 1950s. By the 1970s, the biggest, most spectacular and most famous of the Shows were those held in alternate years at Goroka, in the Eastern Highlands, and Mount Hagen, in the Western Highlands.

An extraordinary amount of work went into the organisation and running of these Highland Shows. Tens of thousands of painted, feathered, decorated tribesmen poured into the towns of Goroka and Mount Hagen over the Show weekends. All had to be housed and fed, and oft-times transported. The highlight of the Show was always the massed dancing; the *sing sings* that were the main attraction for overseas visitors who were fascinated by the kaleidoscope of colour and movement created by the rippling lines of leaping, chanting warriors, and by the pounding rhythm of thousands of hand-drums.

The Goroka Show Committee was determined to make the 1974 Show — the first since PNG gained self-government — one to remember. To

Performing tribesmen at the Highlands Show.

assist the Committee, Bruce Flynn and his advertising men decided to sponsor a stunt guaranteed to thrill the huge crowd of tribesmen who would be present...the first hang-glider to ride the Highlands' skies.

Bill Flewellyn was at this time the World Endurance record holder. His wife, Peggy, was an ex-Australian water ski champion. They often performed at shows and competitions in Australia, and were polished performers. Bill Flewellyn was billed as the Birdman. He dressed the part, and his act was exciting and colourful. His gaily-hued hang-glider was equipped with smoke flares. Towed to a considerable height by a light aircraft, Flewellyn would descend in a series of tight loops and swerves, coloured smoke marking his progress and creating a shifting, dissolving pattern in the sky. The Brewery arranged for the Flewellyns to come to PNG for the Goroka Show.

Before going on to Goroka, Peggy Flewellyn gave a dazzling display of her skill at a water ski marathon, arranged by South Pacific in conjunction with the Port Moresby Water Ski Association. At the Show, Bill Flewellyn's descents from the sky onto the main arena was witnessed by thousands of incredulous tribesmen, open-mouthed with astonishment, which quickly gave way to huge roars of approval. Flewellyn's glider was clothed in the company colours of yellow and green, and carried the SP logo.

So successful was the visit that South Pacific brought Flewellyn back to perform at the Morobe Show, in October. In 1976, Bill Flewellyn appeared again at Goroka under South Pacific sponsorship. His act was even more popular than it had been in 1974.

Although the Birdman was such a hit at the Goroka Show, he could not top an attraction that had created wild excitement in 1973, particularly in the Highlands — the first elephant to come to PNG.

The 'Jumbo the Elephant' promotion was the most successful ever mounted by South Pacific Brewery. Jumbo captured the hearts and imaginations of the Highlanders, and stirred them to frenzies of admiration and delight. To this day, Highlanders remember the visit of Jumbo.

It all started early in 1973. The Secretary of the Department of the Administrator, T.W.Ellis, was paying a visit to his old District, the Western Highlands. Tom Ellis had been a notable District Commissioner, and under his leadership the Western Highlands had rapidly forged ahead. He was a man of strong personality, short of speech and seldom smiling. Nothing mattered to Tom Ellis but the progress of his District. So complete was his domination of local events that he was called 'God' by the irreverent. A story goes that he was once pulled up on the Highlands Highway by a newly arrived young police officer, for speeding. The officer took one look at his catch, blanched, and muttered, 'My God!'. 'Yes, and don't you forget it,' Ellis is said to have grunted as he drove off.

Ellis left the Western Highlands in 1969, but he never missed an opportunity of visiting his favourite part of PNG. On this occasion he was a guest at a meeting of the Mount Hagen Show Committee, at the Pioneers

Right *Star of the 1973 Mount Hagen Highlands Show.*

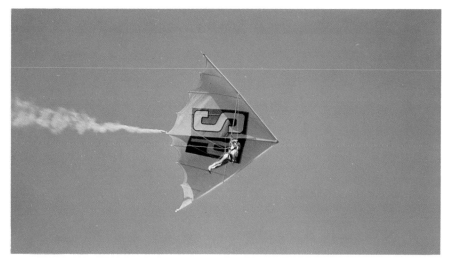

Right and below *Bill Flewellyn soaring the thermals in SP and Anchor colours.*

Club. Ellis had been the inaugural president of the Western Highlands Agricultural Society. Planning was in progress for the forthcoming Show, and the beer was flowing freely. Someone said to Ellis, 'You'll have to come up for the Show, Tom'. Ellis had official commitments and said that he would not be able to attend, whereupon another person is said to have murmured, 'If we can't have God, let's have a bloody elephant!'.

An outrageous idea, but one that grabbed the fancy of the Show Committee. It was spoken in jest, but it was to become reality. The secretary was instructed to write a letter to Bruce Flynn. Could South Pacific come up with an elephant?

Bruce Flynn, too, was captivated by the notion of introducing the mighty elephant to the people of the Western Highlands. It would be a supreme coup for South Pacific Brewery — if it could be brought off. Where was an elephant to be found? Could official permission be obtained to bring an elephant to PNG, and take it out again? What about the cost — it was bound to be considerable? Despite problems popping up on all sides, Bruce Flynn made up his mind that the company was going to bring an elephant to Mount Hagen for the 1973 Show. He instructed Ray Priestley, the marketing manager, to get cracking. Such are the prerogatives of top management.

Priestley did what any sensible man would have done under the circumstances. He passed the buck. He telephoned his regional sales manager in Lae, Noel Mills, and said to him, 'Noel, Bruce Flynn wants an elephant for the Hagen Show. Find us one.'

Mills was appalled. 'My God,' he said. 'Where do I start?' Priestley weakened, and together they began the search for an elephant. Zoos were the logical places to begin, but zoo directors don't like the idea of their precious charges being used for commercial promotions. Circuses have elephants, but they can't afford to part with them. Elephants as a commodity are in rather short supply in Australia, and it began to appear as though Hagen would have an elephantless Show. Then came the breakthrough. Bullen's African Lion Safaris at Beenleigh, in Queensland, were prepared to lend an elephant. It was a lady elephant, but of course she had to be called Jumbo for the Highlands adventure.

So Jumbo began her voyage to PNG, accompanied by her handler, Syd Pridmore. She was an amiable elephant, but sea travel did not agree with her and she lost four hundredweight on the journey. She was shipped on the *Island Chief*, a vessel of the New Guinea Australia Line. 'All discriminating elephants travel NGAL,' boasted an advertisement in the *Post-Courier*.

The forthcoming visit by Jumbo the Elephant made joyous news all over PNG. Popular fancy was tickled by the idea of an elephant as the star of the Mount Hagen Show. Word of the coming of Jumbo flashed through the Highlands. Photographs and descriptions of elephants were distributed; the newspapers and radio programmes made elephants the topic of the day. But the Highlanders had no frame of reference; they gained only the haziest idea of the size and shape of an elephant. Many seemed to think they were

An Eastern Highlander performing at the Highlands Show.

104

Kukukuku tribesmen at Goroka Highlands Show, 1972. (Photo R. J. May).

about to see some kind of giant pig — symbol of wealth and position in the Highlands — with a tail at each end.

The *Island Chief* arrived off Lae on the evening of 20 July, 1973. Noel Mills went out on the pilot's launch with some breakfast for Jumbo — fifty pounds of pumpkins, bales of pawpaw and banana leaves — and remained on board while the ship berthed. Jumbo was swayed onto the wharf in a giant cargo sling, and remained swaying for some little time until she had regained her land-legs. She travelled by low-loader to the Lae Showground, where more than 5,000 cheering Papua New Guineans had gathered to wonder at this mountainous animal, greater by far than their imaginings.

Jumbo remained at the Showground for several weeks, recuperating from her sea voyage. She was closely attended by her trainer and handler, Syd Pridmore, and by officers of the Department of Agriculture, Stock and Fisheries. She was a magnet for the people of Lae, who never tired of watching her every dignified movement. The newspapers carried stories about her size and weight, whetting the appetites of the tribesmen in the Highlands. A 'Colour-in-Competition' was run in the *Post-Courier*, featuring an outline of Jumbo. First prize — a trip for two to the Hagen Show — was won by a young Papuan taxation officer, Ian Kave.

While Jumbo was still in Lae, Bruce Flynn received a telephone call from Paul Cox, executive director of the Tolai Warwagira Festival, Rabaul. South Pacific Brewery, as one of the five major sponsors of the Festival, regularly donated $250 each year towards running costs. This year the Festival Committee had evolved ambitious plans, and Cox asked Flynn if South Pacific would consider becoming a lifetime sponsor by making a donation of $2,500 — ten years' normal contribution, in advance.

'No, we won't do that, Paul,' said Bruce Flynn. 'We'll do something better. How would you like Jumbo to appear at the Festival? The *Island Chief* will be taking her back to Australia after the Hagen Show, and we can offload her at Rabaul on the way. You could have her for a full day. You

Highlands bigman, Wamp Wan rides Jumbo.

should be able to make some money out of her.'

(The offer was accepted. The Festival Committee put Jumbo on display at Elizabeth Park, and charged ten cents admission. Over $3,000 was collected.)

Jumbo's progress to the Hagen Showground along the Highlands Highway from Lae was a triumph. 'We're Trucking It! The Biggest Elephant Truckers in all PNG!', boasted PNG Freighters — Jack Thick's company — in a newspaper advertisement. This was appropriate enough — PNG Freighters were sole transporters for South Pacific Brewery into the Highlands. A big Mack R truck was specially fitted to the requirements of handler Syd Pridmore to accommodate Jumbo in safety and comfort. It was driven by the PNG Freighters Lae operations manager, Ralph Trundell (who later joined South Pacific Brewery). The 'SP Jumbo Convoy' consisted of five vehicles, including the Mack R, and was led by Noel Mills and Bob Robertson, sales representative.

The Highlands Highway runs from Lae through the length of the great Markham Valley, and thence into the Eastern Highlands via the Kassam Pass, on the Markham-Ramu Divide. It traverses the Eastern Highlands and ascends the Daulo Pass into the Chimbu, and the Western Highlands. It connects a string of towns and settlements — Kainantu, Henganofi, Goroka, Asaro, Chuave, Kundiawa, Minj, and many smaller outposts. In these Highlands valleys live approximately 750,000 people. A big percentage were lining the Highway to goggle at Jumbo and her convoy.

Along the route, officers and men of the Royal Papua New Guinea Constabulary were on hand to maintain order, and protect Jumbo from over-enthusiastic admirers. Regular reports on Jumbo's progress were broadcast over ABC Radio. Newspaper notices implored the people to be careful. 'Yu no paitim dispela elephan! Lukaut gut longen!'

'Sapos man in kaikaim abus elephan, bai em i kisim bikpela sik oli kolim elephan bel!', warned one notice, in a jaunty reference to the prevalent Highlands complaint know in Pidgin as 'pig bel', the result of eating tainted pig meat. 'Elephan hia i no wail', another assured, 'emi no save paitim man'.

Accompanying the elephant were ABC and PNG Tourist Board film units, recording this historic event for posterity. Overnight stops were made at Maralume Plantation (owned by Tom Leahy, exparliamentarian and nephew of the famous pioneer Leahy Brothers — Mick, Jim, Dan and Paddy — who did so much to open the Highlands to outside settlement); Yonki, in the Upper Ramu; Kainantu, and Goroka. Brief halts were made at roadside villages. Everywhere Jumbo was greeted by excited Highlanders, who were carried away by the sheer bulk and grandeur of the biggest beast they had ever seen.

Throughout the journey, Jumbo placidly went through her repertoire of tricks and seemed quite unaffected by the tumult around her. She was an old pro, seasoned from years of appearances before audiences of Australian

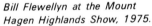
Bill Flewellyn at the Mount Hagen Highlands Show, 1975.

children, and she took the Highlands of Papua New Guinea in her stride.

The author was District Commissioner of the Eastern Highlands when Jumbo arrived at Goroka. The most exaggerated stories of the physical might of the elephant had been flying around the District for days before her arrival. The tribesmen began to assemble in Goroka in huge numbers, pouring into the town on foot and in PMV trucks and Land Cruisers. Every available policeman was on duty to direct the movements of the good-humoured crowd. Popular opinion held that Jumbo was, without doubt, some weird species of pig, and tribesmen wondered whether it was possible to construct a garden fence sufficiently strong to keep out such monsters. One group of grave elders was overheard in a solemn discussion on the ways and means of cooking and butchering such a gigantic beast — what a fearful amount of work would be required to dig an earth oven that was big enough!

At Mount Hagen, Jumbo stole the Show. It is impossible to be certain just how many Highlanders saw her, but certainly there were tens of thousands at the showground alone. The 1973 Hagen Show will for all time be known to the people as the Show of the Elephant.

The Jumbo saga created enormous publicity for South Pacific Brewery, apart from the financial returns enjoyed by the Committees of the Hagen Show and Tolai Warwagira, and the hundreds of small businessmen who sold food, drink and transport to the multitude. Throughout the tour Jumbo was draped in a spectacular cloth in company colours, emblazoned with huge SP letters. The one drawback to the Jumbo promotion was that it was a very hard act to follow.

After returning from her PNG tour, Jumbo remained in quarantine in Taronga Park Zoo, Sydney, for six months. She suffered no ill effects from her adventure.

The final cost of the Jumbo promotion to South Pacific Brewery Ltd. was in excess of $25,000, but all concerned agreed it was money well spent.

12

The Marketing Game

As mentioned in the previous chapter, by the beginning of 1977, the rival brewery had captured almost 15 per cent of the PNG beer market. In April, 1977, San Mig (Swan had dropped out of the venture) released a new range of beers, and stepped up its efforts to cut back the SP lead.

The increased competition from San Mig was naturally of concern to South Pacific. Measures to counter the threat were under constant discussion. SP still had the lion's share of the market, but the resources backing San Mig were so formidable that the company could not afford to rest on its laurels. On 17 November, 1976, the authorised capital of the holding company was increased from 6 million ordinary shares of one kina to 15 million. In December, SP Holdings Ltd. issued 1,983,261 ordinary shares as bonus shares to existing shareholders on a basis of one for three.

In August, 1977, the Board accepted a proposal from Bruce Flynn that the international firm, P.A. Management Services of Knightsbridge, London, be retained to carry out a full review of SP marketing activities. It was apparent that the aggressive marketing approach of San Mig had to be matched, and expert advice was clearly necessary.

The marketing survey was carried out by Tony Dean, who spent six weeks in Papua New Guinea. Before returning to London, Dean discussed his findings with Bruce Flynn. The key recommendation he would make in his report, said Dean, was for the appointment of a manager of SP's overall marketing operation.

In December, 1977, P.A.Marketing Services placed a number of advertisements in a range of newspapers for a 'marketing executive, Papua New Guinea'. One was read by Ken A.Webb, in his home at Hertfordshire, thirty miles outside North London.

Ken Webb was at that time employed as marketing director of the British branch of a large American company. He was comfortably settled with his wife and family and had a rewarding job, but England is a cold, damp place in winter and although Webb knew nothing of PNG — he had

Canoe racing, a popular PNG sport. Such clubs are sponsored by SP Brewery.

109

only the haziest idea of its location — he knew it was in the hot tropics; an appealing thought. After discussing the matter with his wife, Carol, Ken Webb applied for the position. He was interviewed by Bruce Flynn in London, and was offered a four-year appointment, which he accepted. But some time passed before the Webbs arrived in Port Moresby.

It was no longer possible for a company in PNG to employ expatriates at will. The government of an independent PNG wanted as many positions as possible to be filled by citizens, and required each foreign company to develop an approved training and localisation programme for its Papua New Guinean employees. The provisions of the *National Investment and Development Act* obliged all existing foreign enterprises — which under the definition contained in the Act included South Pacific Brewery Ltd. — to register with NIDA, the National Investment and Development Authority. This authority was established by the government to channel and control foreign business activities into fields consistent with national policies and goals, and to facilitate Papua New Guinean participation in investment and in the ownership and management of foreign enterprises. At the same time many occupations were reserved for Papua New Guineans alone. Employers were forbidden to engage overseas persons in a work category declared reserved, without express approval. As time went by, the list of reserved occupations grew, although PNG required (and in 1982, still does) overseas expertise in a large number of specialised fields.

The position to be occupied by Ken Webb was certainly not reserved, but it was still necessary for South Pacific to follow rigid procedures before permission to employ him could be obtained. An application had to be made to the Department of Labour and Industry for a work permit, and to the Department of Foreign Affairs for a visa. In support of the application for a work permit, the company was required to furnish a considerable amount of information. This included a copy of the approved training and localisation programme, a full and explicit manning and establishment schedule of the entire SP organisation, the names of national apprentices and trainees, full details of the proposed employee, and whether or not he was a replacement, or an addition. The passing of the *Non-Citizens Employment Act* 1980 has since made it even more difficult for companies like South Pacific to engage overseas staff.

Ken Webb arrived at Port Moresby with his family in July, 1978. His position was at first designated 'Marketing Manager, Strategies'. Ray Priestley became Marketing Manager, Sales Administration. At the end of 1979, Webb was placed in overall control of marketing, with the title 'Group Marketing Controller'.

The job was no sinecure. The marketing of beer is a tricky proposition. Consumer tastes cannot always be predicted, and it is hard to wean a confirmed beer drinker from his favourite brew.

Since beginning beer production, a number of beers, bottle types and labels had been introduced by South Pacific. South Pacific Lager, the first

Ken Webb, Group Marketing Controller.

beer brewed, was sold in a red-labelled bottle from 1952 to 1964. In 1953, SP draught in bottles, and Export Lager, appeared and remained on the market for many years. South Pacific Lager Export Special in brown bottles — soon commonly referred to as 'Brownies' — was introduced in 1962, and Gold Medal Lager in green bottles — 'Greenies' — two years later. Golden Lager, promoted extensively in 1954 and 1955, did not catch on and was dropped from the production line, and Anchor brand, too, failed in the market place despite an intensive sales effort and the expenditure of $75,000 in advertising.

Green bottles were first used by South Pacific during the slump of the late 1950s and early 1960s referred to in chapter five. To keep costs under control, Bill Johns had been forced to look for second-hand bottles, and he found them in Hollandia, Dutch New Guinea. They were long-necked green Heineken bottles, different in shape and colour from anything

Tabubil Airport; light aircraft provide the only means of visiting some of the remote areas of Papua New Guinea.

The new 'Brownie and Greenie' take-home packs with rip-off tops.

previously used, and the company purchased them with reluctance. But they were an instant hit with the drinker, and green bottles of one kind or another have remained in use, with brown, ever since.

There was no doubting the quality of SP beer. On the two occasions that the company had entered its beer in international exhibitions — in 1964 and 1967, at Brussels — they were awarded gold medals for quality (hence the introduction of 'Gold Medal Lager' in PNG in 1964).

In 1974, the advertising consultants, Brainsell, were appointed advertising agents to the company for a period of twelve months. Planning began to develop the 'greenie' and 'brownie' beers, in bottles and cans, as the sole SP packaged brands. The rip-top principle of closure was adopted in May, 1978. The production capacity of the Lae brewery was expanded to 6.6 million gallons per year just before the 1975 fire, and the reconstruction forced by that catastrophe resulted in another lift, to 7,250,000 gallons, by the time Webb became Group Marketing Controller.

The South Pacific production capacity was clearly in a healthy condition. It was Ken Webb's job to marry this capacity with the marketing side, and fight off the developing San Mig challenge.

The marketing operation had been continually evolving since the early days of the company. Lines of communication in a physically huge and diverse country like PNG were long and frequently difficult. At first, SP beer had been freely available only in Port Moresby and outlying districts, and distribution presented no particular problem. As sales of SP spread throughout PNG, however, difficulties multiplied.

Over the years, a chain of depots and stockists was developed, covering the whole country. By the time of Ken Webb's arrival, PNG had been divided into three SP sales regions. Region one covered Papua, with a depot at Daru and stockists at Samarai and Popondetta. Region two was mainland New Guinea, with depots at Lae, Bulolo, Goroka, Mount Hagen, Madang and Wewak, and stockists at Vanimo and Aitape. Region three covered the Islands, with depots at Kavieng, Kimbe, Rabaul, and Kieta, and with stockists at Manus and Buka. It was South Pacific policy to replace stockists with a depot operation when turnover reached a sufficiently high point. Regions were in charge of regional sales managers. In 1978, they were Gerry Faramus in region one, Bob Robertson in region two, and Stan Neal in region three. Each region also had an area manager.

These depots and stockists were supplied with the aid of a large fleet of vehicles (over 200 were operated by SP alone, and contractors were also used), coastal shipping (South Pacific was the largest single user of the coastal fleet, shipping around 80,000 cubic metres per year) and on occasion by aircraft. The company had fixed assets scattered all over PNG. A multitude of clubs and hotels used SP-supplied refrigerators, coolrooms and beer dispensers. By 1978, there were 912 liquor licences in force in PNG. Of these, forty-two were publicans' licences, twenty-one tavern, twenty-one limited hotel, forty-two restaurant, 172 club, sixty-one dealers', fifty bottleshop, three canteen, and 500 storekeepers'. The total number of licences had risen to 1,223 by mid-1979, the principal increase being in storekeepers' licences.

At a meeting in Port Moresby in late October, 1981, Jim Cromie, Bill Johns, Lloyd Hurrell and Bruce Flynn talked with the author of the early years, recalling personalities and events that helped to shape the history of South Pacific Brewery Ltd. The American airmen stationed in Port Moresby in the early 1960s who used to purchase kegs of SP, load them into the bomb-bays of their B17 bombers, and fly off on long geophysical missions, at great altitudes. Upon landing, the kegs were ice-cold, and ready for immediate drinking.

Florence Gilmore, who with her husband, Jack, ran the old Madang Hotel. She once complained that sixty kegs of SP draught had gone bad.

SP Brewery display in Steamships store, Port Moresby.

The Gilmores were good customers, and Bill Johns himself attended to the complaint. He found that Flo and Jack were storing their beer outside, in the fierce tropical sun, and were not rotating the kegs. Some had been standing for six months and more, and no beer will take that sort of treatment. And draught beer, unlike bottled, was not pasteurised.

On another occasion in the late 1950s, Flo Gilmore complained about the quality of the SP draught beer, and this time Bruce Flynn went to Madang to check things out. He found that the beer lines, extractors and taps needed cleaning and servicing, and he quickly put matters right. Flo was pleased, but then she said, 'Bruce, those refrigerators SP have supplied us are no good'.

'Why is that?' Flynn asked.

'Well, every morning when I check them, they're hot!'

Bruce Flynn knew that Jack Gilmore hated to waste expensive electricity. 'Flo,' he said, 'you go to bed pretty early, don't you?'

'Yes,' Flo replied.

'Well, you get up tonight at about a quarter to ten, and come with me and we'll follow Jack.'

That night, they tiptoed around the Madang Hotel after Jack as he furtively switched off every refrigerator.

'Didn't she blow him up!' Bruce Flynn told the meeting. They went on to exchange stories of Leonard McEachern and others, Hamac Holdings and sundry business dealings, unfortunately unpublishable but part of the commercial history of Papua New Guinea. Stories of Dorothy Stewart in her nightie, chastising a merry Bill Johns and Bruce Flynn, noisily riding pushbikes up and down the corridors of the Ascot Hotel in the wee hours after day-long sessions with customers. 'She was the greatest sight you ever saw,' Johns said fondly. 'She tore strips off us for disturbing the guests...' They recalled the names and exploits of hoteliers and managers known throughout PNG — men like John Peterson, Reg Eginton, Fletcher Hayes, John Pitt, the gigantic Bert Gassman, Bob Zeelan — a Dutchman who cooked with the inspired touch of an angel, but was not so hot as a hotel manager, Wal Morrisey — long time mine host of the Boroko Hotel, and Tom Abberton. Abberton was an outstanding publican, manager in turn of the Goroka and Madang Hotels, the Highlander at Mount Hagen, the Melanesian at Lae, and the Gateway at Port Moresby. He had a good war record, and found time to serve as president of the Goroka Rotary Club, chairman of the Goroka Town Advisory Council and member of the Eastern Highlands District Advisory Council.

The development of the South Pacific marketing network was another topic discussed at that October gathering.

'Getting our beer into the Highlands was hard at first, before the Highway was opened,' Bruce Flynn recalled. 'We used to ship it from Moresby to Madang, and then fly it in to Goroka at twopence per pound, and to Hagen for fourpence. Expensive beer by the time it landed. Then about

Early SP Brewery labels.

1963 Jack Thick came along to see me at Lae. He said to me, "Why are you flying that beer in? I'll take it for you by road. It'll be a lot cheaper."

I said, "Jack, the road's not open yet."

"Of course the road's bloody open," Jack snorted. So we worked out a freight rate and from that time on, until he sold his PNG Freighters a year or two ago, Jack hauled all our beer into the Highlands. The road wasn't officially opened until 1965, but he always got it through. Bob Robertson has a photo of Jack with 199 blokes behind him, each carrying an eighty-litre keg across a slip in Daulo Pass. He took about a week to ferry thousands of litres of beer across that slip to trucks waiting on the Hagen side. "I told you the bloody road was open," Jack said to me. New Guinea Transport bought Jack Thick out — John Nilkare is on their Board — and they still carry SP beer into the Highlands.'

'We've had a very long and happy association with Collins and Leahy,' Bill Johns said. 'They have been major agents of ours in the Highlands for many years. Bobby Gibbes sold a lot of our beer in his chain of pubs, too. Tang Mau is our agent in Wewak. Eventually we bought land there, and it is one of the places where we own our own depot, instead of leasing it. We used to sell our beer through stockists at Popondetta, but now we have a depot there, too.'

'Ron Neville was our agent at Mendi for years,' Flynn recalled. 'Brian Heagney is an agent for San Mig now, but he was ours for many years in the Chimbu. We had Graham Pople at Tufi for a long time — he left about a year ago.' [All were ex-government officers, who resigned and became businessmen. Both Neville and Pople were once elected members of the House of Assembly and Brian Heagney is still one of the best known expatriates in the Highlands.] 'We leased a depot at Alotau from Freddie Craig, but for the last couple of years our agents have been the business arm of the Provincial Government — Milne Bay Development Corporation.'

'We went into Samarai through stockists — BP's and Steamships,' Bill Johns added. 'In New Ireland, BP's were our agents until they joined with the Asahi Breweries people to start Territory United, then we set up our own depot. Today, we rent premises from the Provincial Government. When Mick Gallen [ex-police officer and well-known sportsman, who resigned to become a publican] was at Namatanai, we supplied him direct.

'Rabaul was the interesting place. Our first depot was established there. Both Madang — where Bill McKenzie has been our agent for years — and Rabaul were dyed-in-the-wool Victoria Bitter towns — some drinkers just wouldn't look at anything else. Even the likes of Arthur Brown used to say to me, "It's no good, Bill. You'll never get them off VB". It took us a long time to get our beer into Rabaul. After prohibition was lifted, the Chinese became the big liquor traders in Rabaul. We couldn't get them to handle our beer until Neville Barnes — he was N.E.Barnes Trading Company — became our representative. He knew the Rabaul Chinese pretty well, and soon SP beer was being sold right through the Gazelle.

The coconut palm is an integral part of the SP symbol. This palm stands protected in the heart of the Lae Brewery heavy vehicle access road; 'Woe betide any careless driver'.

'Arthur Brown sold an awful lot of SP after prohibition. He built a new bar at the Ascot for the Papua New Guinean trade. It must have been fifty yards long. An enormous thing. We delivered beer by semi-trailer, a thousand cartons at a time!'

The first travelling sales representative of South Pacific Brewery Ltd. was Roy McKain. As mentioned in chapter five, McKain joined the company as a clerk, in 1953. A lean, alert man with a dry sense of humour, Roy McKain was living in retirement in Brisbane when interviewed by the author in April, 1982.

'I first went to New Guinea in September, 1951, to Manus Island, to work for the Commonwealth Department of Works,' McKain recalled. 'Then I went over to Works and Housing, as a storeman-timekeeper. When I joined SP as a clerk, it was a very small show — just Rudi Meier as general manager-brewmaster, Johnny Nydam, Ernie Fletcher in charge of the bottling hall, a Polish joker in the workshop, about twenty-five Keremas, and Bill Young and me in the office. That was it. We only brewed three days a week, and bottled on two.

'Rudi Meier was a very strange man. Most of the time he got about in trousers with shoes and socks, but no shirt. He used weird building methods, but they seemed to work! After a bit Bill Young left, and I replaced him. They called me the accountant, but I wasn't an accountant — I was just a clerk. I suppose it looked better on the company books. Meier lived with his little Swiss wife in the house at the brewery, and the office was underneath. Not much of an office — just an old typewriter, a telephone and a desk. We weren't getting too many orders then; Carlton and United were making things tough.

'In those days we sold our bottled beer with red and blue labels. Red was the regular lager, and the other was export. Same beer, but . . . . . If an order came in for red and we were out of it, we'd just soak off blue labels in a forty-four gallon drum and slap on red. Nobody ever noticed the difference.

'Everything in the brewery then was second hand and patched up. Didn't have the modern bottling and cleaning machinery we have today, and of course the bottles were sometimes dirty, even after the boys had swabbed them out one at a time with hand brushes. Labour was cheap then. Customers sometimes complained, and Meier would say to me, "Give them a dozen free bottles!" A few jokers worked a nice little racket, dirtying up clean bottles after they'd drunk them, and getting free replacements. We woke up, but.

'The first refrigeration units we got hold of were old Coldstream Temprites, motor driven and water cooled. They were cows of things to service. We put them in the clubs in Port Moresby, and Johnny Nydam used to go round and clean the lines, extractors and taps. If they weren't kept clean, the draught beer would get dirty and yeasty, and the customers

GRASS ROOTS

NO..No...ITSSS ...SSSNOT TRUE...HE BLARY CHEATED AND.. HIC..!! AND BOUGHT THE F..FIRSST ONE..

...BURP!!..MY ..ULT...HE..HE.. FORCED TO GET SSPARK...

Rival brewers SP and San Mig yesterday slashed 27 per cent from the current retail price of their products.

As in their earlier "war," in which a truce was supposed to have been agreed in June, each side blamed the other for starting it.

would bitch. After a while they gave this job to me. I'd go out and flush the lines out with a caustic mixture, then with water. Dangerous if you didn't get rid of all the caustic.

'We didn't bother much then about formalities. There was a club on Paga Hill that was supposed to have a Temprite installed, and the manager rang me and said it hadn't been delivered. But it had. Johnny Nydam had gone up there on Sunday afternoon when the club was closed, removed the hasp and staple and lock from the front door, gone in, hacked away a part of the bar so the Temprite would fit, started her up, then screwed it all together again. The manager threatened to sue him for breaking and entering. That was Johnny Nydam.

'Anyway, after Heinekens and MBL came in, Rudi Meier was unhappy. He liked to do things his way, so he and Nydam went off to Lae and started Guinea Brewery. Bill Johns took over as general manager of SP, and things began to change. I went out on the road, and that's where I stayed.

'It was hard to get around PNG then. There was no road into the Highlands, and boat and plane movements were pretty erratic. I'd often be away for three weeks. Bill Johns and me 'd work out different sales trips, and off I'd go. The hotels were pretty crook, and you'd often have to share a room. Hard to get your washing done when you were constantly moving. I used to carry a big tin of Johnson's Baby Powder, to make wearing dirty shirts a bit easier. Slap some some down your front and back, and she'd be right.

'I remember when prohibition was lifted. Johnsie got all excited, and he said to me, "Roy, here's a great chance to sell our beer. Let's get a boat from BP's, load it up with beer, and you can flog it to the coastal villagers between here and Lae. They'll be waiting with their money in their hands!"

'Well, I wasn't so sure about that, but Johnsie was the boss. So we loaded 10,000 cartons onto a Burns Philp K boat, and one Sunday night off we went.

'Those K boats were typical of the coasters operating then. About two hundred tons, with a white master, engineer and bosun and a Papua New Guinean crew. The one we were on was the *Kurwina*. The skipper was Jim McCormack, and he was a shrewd one. I had to share a cabin with a drunk. He snored all night, and there were millions of cockroaches, so big you could have put a saddle on 'em. I didn't sleep a wink.

'Next morning we made our first stop, somewhere east of Moresby. Just hove to off a white sandy beach — no sign of any buildings — and launched a surfboat, loaded up with cargo. All sorts of groceries and stuff, including perishables, bread and freezer meat and that. A pinnace towed the surfboat in. Near the shore the waves got her, and over she went. The lot went into the drink. The skipper said, "Right, now we'll try your beer".

'"Not bloody likely," I said to him. "I'm not going to send in forty cartons through that surf. I'd lose it!". I thought to myself, "poor bloody people on the outstations. What a way to live."

Hey mate, hic . . . . don't you want to help the poor breweries increase their sales . . . . .
Later, bro! When they bring it down to five bucks, then I'll start again . . . . .

The price of San Miguel beer goes down 61 toea a carton today as the big Filipino brewery continues its market assault on local competitor SP.

'Well, the weather was good and it was a nice cruise. We sat on deck in the sun and drank beer, but did we sell any? Not likely. Johnsie had it all wrong. Those village people just weren't interested in our beer. I don't know why — they were socking it away in the towns. I think I sold twenty cartons out of that 10,000 — and we drank forty.

'The food was lousy, too. Jim McCormack had a big freezer full of good *kai*, stuff like roasts and chops and chooks and sausages, but we get any of it? We did not. He served us muck like curried liver and rice. We caught plenty of fish on that trip, but we got none of that, either. They told me in Samarai that Jim and the bosun used to flog the freezer and fish. They made a good thing of it. In Samarai, I laid in my own supply of cheese, biscuits, butter, salami sausage, tinned beans and asparagus, to see me through to Lae. Curried liver? God. I was pleased to get off that boat.

'I was on the road from '55 to '80. As we got bigger and shipping and transport improved, we started to build depots. The first was at Rabaul. That was before we bought the Lae brewery. We leased Mack Foley's old garage, on Mango Avenue opposite Elizabeth Park. Lance Ellis was sent there, to service the great big coolroom we installed. Our draught beer wasn't pasteurised, and it'd only last four to six weeks unless it was held in a coldroom. With shipping the way it was then we'd send over, say, 200 kegs at a time, plus the bottled stuff. Lance wasn't a salesman. BP's handled all our sales in Rabaul then, all the paperwork and administration. Lance just had to look after the coldroom, and the beer dispensers in the clubs and pubs.

'I helped out there for a month in the late 'fifties. We both had to wipe off the kegs before Arthur Brown would have them in his bar. Lance was still servicing old Temprite units, and he asked me if I'd like to do the rounds with him. "We'll leave at six in the morning," Lance said.

'"Why so early," says I.

'"Sometimes we have early morning drinkers in the clubs," he says.

'"Don't be silly," I said. "You're having me on."

But he wasn't. The first club we went to was the old Yacht Club, and there's ten or fifteen jokers sitting round, drinking things like rum and creme-de-menthe, as well as beer. The manager was behind the bar, counting his money and that. All those blokes were skippers and engineers from the traders and copra boats in the harbour. Their ships were loading or unloading and there was nothing for them to do, so they'd come to the Yacht Club for an hour or two, then up to the RSL, then on to the Ascot when the pubs opened, down to the Cosmo, the New Guinea Club, then back here for a nightcap before going back to their boats. Mind you, not many of them drank at sea, but they made up for it on land.

'Later on, I went to Rabaul as the rep-manager after BP's relinquished their SP contract, and we set up a proper depot.

'When Ken Webb took over, I was regional sales manager for the Papua region. Webby was reorganising things, and they made me advertising

Never mind . . . . . leave it . . . . . .
they're only bloody greenies . . .
I like the expensive ones . . .

More than K9000 worth of beer was stolen from a stranded truck near Watabung on the Highlands Highway this week.

manager not that I knew anything about advertising. After Webby became group marketing controller, Ray Priestley left, and in March, 1980, I left too. PNG was changing too fast for me, so I retired and came down here to live. I always got on well with Bruce Flynn, and he gave me a trip to London and Istanbul before I went. Oh, that was great, but Australia'll do me now.'

After Ken Webb became group marketing controller, region two — all of mainland New Guinea — was split into regions two and four. The rapid spread of village clubs, particularly in the Highlands, combined with the proliferation of licensed outlets previously mentioned made the region too big for one man to adequately handle. The new region four covered the Highlands and Madang; region two handled the rest of the mainland. Region two was taken over by Neil Robinson, while Bob Robertson looked after four. Gerry Faramus, who had been manager of region one, took over as advertising manager after Roy McKain departed, and subsequently became national sales manager. Ray Thompson replaced him in region one.

In 1973, South Pacific Brewery Ltd. formed a Management Services section within the Marketing and Sales Division. The aim was to make management skills and staff training available to national groups, companies and individuals who wanted to enter the liquor industry and operate their own hotels, clubs and taverns. The recent move by provincial governments and local government councils into the industry has resulted in increasing calls being made on the South Pacific Management Services section.

Many national business enterprises in PNG fail because of ignorance of fundamentals. Few Papua New Guineans have been educated in such ordinary business skills as basic accounting, pricing, stock control and so on. Without help, their businesses quickly founder.

Through its Management Services section, South Pacific today provides a range of services; initial feasibility studies, design, renovation and equipment advice, financial planning, a staff recruitment and training service, stocking advice and trading supervision. These are provided free, or at cost. Management and accountancy fees are charged once a new enterprise is in operation, if these services are required.

A number of nationally-owned small hotels and taverns have been set up with the assistance of the South Pacific Management Services section. Some of these enterprises are owned by the business arms of provincial governments. South Pacific is often called upon to provide a manager in the early stages of a new operation, and provides relieving managers on request. On such occasions, the outlet pays the manager's salary.

Hotels that have been managed by South Pacific include the Lorengau, the Boroko, the Wapen at Maprik and the Kepa Tavern, Wapenamanda. Many smaller outlets — police clubs, the Lae Rugby League club, the Lae Miscellaneous Workers Club, for example — have availed themselves of the service. Dobien Kapi of the Management Services section has been an out-

119

standingly successful relieving manager.

One of the recommendations in the P.A. Management Services report was concerned with the need for South Pacific to evolve marketing techniques that would specifically appeal to the principal customer, the Papua New Guinean drinker. The report had concluded that the company was in some danger of losing touch with this vital part of the market.

The off-premises beer advertising ban sharply limited the options open to South Pacific, and also San Mig. Following the imposition of the ban, both companies agreed that each would limit advertising to the use of company names and logos. As time went by and competition between the rival breweries intensified, the mutually agreed policy was gradually abandoned. Both breweries began to develop on-premises promotions for their respective beers, sailing as close to the wind as they felt was prudent.

Particularly successful was the South Pacific sponsorship of the GWADUS group, a band of young Papua New Guinea musicians. They appeared one day in Ken Webb's office, seeking financial backing. They were enthusiastic young people, and skilled instrumentalists. Official policy favoured the provision of musical entertainment in public bars. This was seen to be a calming influence on the patrons, and the Minister for Correctional Services and Liquor Licensing, Mrs Nahau Rooney, her successors, Delba Biri and Akepa Miakwe, and the Chief Licensing Commissioner, W. Tagau, all supported the concept.

The Gwadus group performing.

South Pacific Brewery came to an agreement with the GWADUS group. The brewery supplied them with the finest musical instruments and necessary electrical equipment. The cost — some K3,000 — was deducted in small amounts over a period of time from performing fees paid to the group. The GWADUS group performed — and still does — in hotel bars and clubs throughout PNG, and accepted outside bookings. They have become one of PNG's most popular instrumental groups, and they are still sponsored exclusively by South Pacific.

Shortly before Ken Webb's arrival in PNG, Bruce Flynn went on a holiday to the United States of America. There he encountered the genial American custom of exchanging wishes for a nice or happy day. He felt that 'Have a Happy Day' would be a most appropriate slogan for SP, and one that could hardly be held to offend against the advertising ban.

'Have a Happy Day' was pushed energetically by the SP marketing team after Webb's arrival. The slogan, surrounded by the South Pacific colours of green and yellow, was soon encountered all over PNG.

Recently, pig raffles have become highly popular with PNG beer drinkers. The pig, of course, holds an honoured place in the esteem of the PNG people. As much a symbol of wealth and position as meat, possession of many pigs brings particular satisfaction to the Papua New Guinean.

'Have a Happy Day'.

South Pacific introduced live pig raffles for the first time in Lae, at the

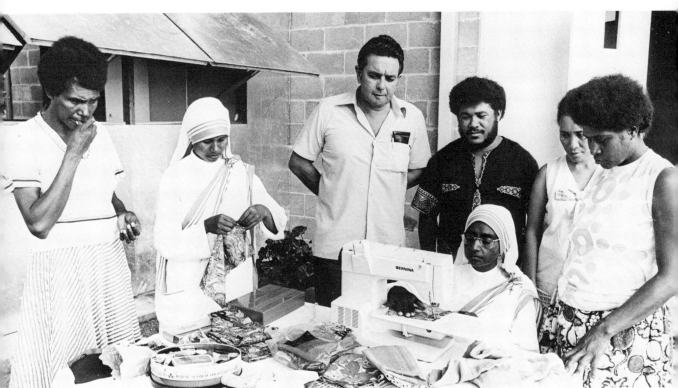

GRASS ROOTS

EH BAMAN!/.. KISIM
WANPELA S........
EH SORI!.. WANPELA
BRAUNPELA BOTOL
I GAT YUNOWANEM-
SAMTING I STAP
INSAIT.. PLIS...

*Hey barman . . . . . bring one
bottle of S . . . . .
Sorry . . . . . one brown bottle
with you-know-what inside,
please.*

The Liquor Licensing Commission has warned it may be forced to take stronger action against people who disobey the law on liquor advertising.

Top Left *Operation Drake
exploration team members,
with their 'necessary supplies',
1980.*
Left *Presentation of four sewing
machines to the Sisters of
Charity for their village projects.*

Cecil, Flora Stewart's old hotel. She had long since — in July, 1957 — sold the Cecil, which became a part of the Morobe Hotels group and later underwent other ownership changes. Mrs Stewart herself died in Lae in May, 1979, at the grand old age of ninety-two.

As noted previously, Mrs Nahau Rooney was an unusually dedicated Minister, and she kept a close eye on the advertising policies of both South Pacific and San Mig. Early in her reign she locked horns with Bruce Flynn and his marketing team. She had grave doubts about the South Pacific 'Have a Happy Day' slogan, considering that it had become synonymous with South Pacific Brewery and SP beer. In June, 1978, she wrote to Flynn, accusing the company of circumventing the government's intentions by using the concept of sponsorship of sport to entice the people to drink beer. 'Whereas previously the public was told that "beer is good", now they are told "SP is good". Before, the message was that sportsmen needed beer, now the message is that sportsmen need and rely on SP. Similarly, the practice of painting licenced trade stores and other buildings in green and yellow is just as persuasive as writing the word "beer" all over the building...'

South Pacific had always prided itself on its strict observance of the law of the land. Bruce Flynn defended the company's practices, and sought further clarification of the less-than-specific advertising rules. 'Our outside advertising has always been one of corporate identification, and on premise, brand identification,' he wrote to Mrs Rooney.

Discussions followed, and at the request of the Minister the company submitted a complete schedule of the various sporting bodies and associations it had assisted during the 1977/78 financial year. It made memorable reading. During this typical year, the company supported seventy-six sporting bodies engaged in thirty-five different sports in all nineteen provinces of PNG, both in cash and in kind — uniforms, footballs, basketballs, goalposts, labour, programmes, trophies, prizes, badges, banners, posters, advertisements and so on. The community service and sports guides in the newspapers were continued. The total value of this assistance — for international, national, provincial and club events — was at least K74,000. In addition, sponsorship of various cultural and educational events ran to another K17,000. Other, uncosted assistance totalled an estimated K18,000.

There were no strings attached to this assistance, although the company did ask the sporting body concerned to allow it to advertise to the general public that the assistance had been given. Teams assisted were asked to play, if possible, in SP colours.

The range of events supported by South Pacific Brewery Ltd. was quite extraordinary. Many of the sports concerned were listed in a previous chapter. During the 1977/78 year, the company sponsored an international golf tournament, several international football events, the PNG Challenge World Half Ton Cup yacht race, a world championship squash tournament, and other prestige encounters. Assistance was given to service clubs

123

— Rotary, Lions, Apex — the Red Cross, and all kinds of show associations, charities and community groups.

That financial support from breweries and tobacco companies was still vital to sports administration, was indicated by letters published in the correspondence pages of the newspapers. Typical was one from Laurie Mills, captain of the Boroko RSL Gun Club, published in July, 1978 —

'As with most sporting bodies in PNG, our club operates within a very fine money margin...the assistance we receive from the breweries, while small compared to their generous support to other sporting bodies, does help us to survive and keep our annual subscriptions and fees to a reasonable level...without this support, annual fees may rise to a level where a great number of people could not afford to play sport. This would be detrimental of PNG...'.

Mrs Rooney was impressed by the extent of SP help to the sporting and

Below *Preparation of the cavalcade, that went through Port Moresby prior to the SP Brewery-sponsored World Title fight, November 1979, between John Aba and Eusebio Pedroza.*

general community. In October, 1978, a notice in the *National Gazette* gave approval for South Pacific and other companies to use company names, symbols, colours and brand names on buildings, cars, trucks, and equipment used for production, distribution and storage, and on company stationery, cartons, kegs, and on giveaway items such as bar trays and chits, ashtrays, coasters, glasses, game boards and so on.

The notice was imperfectly drafted, and companies like South Pacific have since found it difficult to avoid conflict with advertising guidelines. Following a request by Mrs Rooney, all SP signs, hoardings, posters and billboards throughout PNG not on licenced premises were painted out by mid-1979.

Mrs Nahau Rooney was succeeded as Minister for Correctional Services and Liquor Licensing by Delba Biri, following a celebrated and widely discussed disagreement with the judges of the National Court that resulted in the gaoling of Mrs Rooney on charges of contempt of court, and her immediate release by order of Prime Minister Somare. The new Minister soon indicated that he was prepared to allow sponsorship of sport to continue, but under proper controls.

The sport of boxing was lately becoming popular in PNG. San Mig had been sponsoring the talented fighter, Martin Beni, since the early 1970s to considerable public acclaim, and assisted other sports — particulary rugby league and wrestling — although on a lesser scale than SP. By early 1976, San Mig was advertising its product as 'The Sportsman's Beer', an affront to South Pacific. San Mig began a 'Sportsman of the Month' national competition in 1977.

Martin Beni was an established favourite with the PNG public, but he failed to win a major crown, and dropped out of the public eye. South Pacific took under its wing another up-and-coming boxer, John Aba. A featherweight, Aba was probably the best prospect for a world title so far produced by PNG. In 1979, the reigning world featherweight champion, Eusebio Pedroza of Panama, agreed to fight John Aba in Port Moresby for the title — the first professional world boxing championship contest ever to be held in Papua New Guinea.

South Pacific Brewery Ltd. applied to the Minister for approval to promote the big fight, in conjunction with Aba Promotions and the tobacco company, W.D.& H.O.Wills. Permission was granted, provided, the Minister said sternly, South Pacific did not 'use this privilege as an excuse to promote beer'. On the other hand, the government came to the party by guaranteeing K100,000 of the K120,000 that was to be paid to Pedroza on a win-or-lose basis.

The big fight was staged in the Sir Hubert Murray Stadium on Saturday, 17 November, 1979, to enormous acclaim. There was genuine international interest in the battle. The Brisbane TV Channel Seven sent a production team to Port Moresby to capture the event on film.

Sir Hubert Murray Stadium, venue for the World Featherweight title fight, John Aba versus Eusebio Pedroza of Panama.

The odds had to favour the world champion. In twenty-seven professional fights he had won fifteen by knock-out, and nine by judges' decisions. He had lost fights by knock-out on three occasions only, and only once in his career had he been extended to the fifteen-round limit. He had met and defeated some of the gamest scrappers in the business. John Aba was a strong fighter, but he lacked world experience. Under the direction of trainer Norm Salter he trained hard, assisted by former world lightweight champion Gabriel 'Flash' Elorde, from the Philippines. Some experts rated Aba's chances as excellent, but one Port Moresby bookmaker had Pedroza at six to one on, and Aba at two to one.

The event went by the book. John Aba was defeated, but he was not disgraced. He put up a stout fight and stayed for eleven rounds, the best performance to date by any of Pedroza's challengers. The fight ended on a controversial note, with John Aba being pushed in the heat of the battle while he was off balance. He fell through the ropes, hitting his head with a sickening thud on a metal stanchion. The doctor recommended his retirement from the fight.

Unfortunately, the high prizemoney dictated equally high admission charges — K6 to K100 — and despite massive publicity by South Pacific Brewery and its co-promoters, attendance was poor and the gate returns resulted in an overall loss. The government was asked to provide K78,000 in accordance with its guarantee. Some cash was received from the sale of a video film of the fight, but the government's fingers were severely burned.

It was, of course, wonderful publicity for South Pacific. True to its undertaking, the company made no attempt to use the occasion to promote beer, but the publicity spin-off was immense.

South Pacific Brewery continues to sponsor sport, and community and cultural activities in Papua New Guinea.

13

Towards the Future

In the previous chapter, brief mention was made of the emphasis now being placed by the Papua New Guinea Government on the training of nationals to take over management positions in foreign-owned companies. All such companies have been required to develop approved training and localisation programmes, and are expected to place nationals in management positions as rapidly as possible.

The current South Pacific programme was prepared by David Tarrant, an ex-officer of the Department of Labour of Australian colonial times, who was commissioned by the company to undertake the task. Covering the period 1980-1985, the programme has been accepted by the govenment. It is updated annually.

At 30 November, 1980, a total of 950 persons were employed by South Pacific in five major divisions: Marketing and Sales, Production and Engineering, Personnel, Finance and Administration, and Secretarial (including Computer Services and Internal Audit). Of these, 886 were citizens of PNG. It was intended to reduce the number of non-citizens employed at that time from sixty-four to forty-one by the end of 1985. During the period 1976-1980, the establishment of non-citizens had in fact remained constant, although there had been an overall staff growth of 44 per cent.

At 31 December, 1981, the company was substantially on target. The number of expatriates then employed had fallen to forty-seven, out of a total staff that had been streamlined to 821.

The bald figures tell only a part of the story. As early as May, 1967, the South Pacific Board had formally adopted a policy of employing competent nationals as replacements for expatriates, wherever they could be recruited. By this time it was becoming obvious that constitutional change was going to occur in PNG sooner rather than later, and it was but prudent to plan for the future. From the early 1970s onwards, the SP management had carried out an annual review of training requirements for all staff, national and overseas.

SP's Port Moresby Brewery.

Unfortunately, and for reasons considered in an earlier chapter, educated Papua New Guineans were few and far between in the middle 1960s and at first the company was able to recruit only a handful with higher training potential. Demand far exceeded supply. The situation improved as more and more Administration, secondary and technical schools were opened, and some outstanding young nationals are today employed by South Pacific. It remains a truism, however, that the process of localisation can be hurried only up to a point. A certain standard of efficiency must be maintained in any enterprise, if it is to survive. Over-rapid localisation will benefit neither South Pacific nor Papua New Guinea.

Apart from apprenticeships, the earliest attempts by South Pacific to train Papua New Guineans were by in-house instruction. This was successful in many individual cases, in lower-level positions. Following the appointment of the first South Pacific training officer, W.T.Barclay, in-house training courses of many kinds were developed. In 1966 a course was held for ten national foremen and supervisors, aided by officers of the Department of Labour. In 1967 the first of a regular series of courses was given, covering simple English, introductory brewing and the job of laboratory assistant. Barmanship courses, too, were held. These were very popular, and have continued to the present day. Early courses were of one month's duration. Clubs and hotels were invited to nominate national bar employees, for uniform training. In recent years the barmanship courses

128

have been concentrated into five days, and cover stock control and the dispensing of wines and spirits as well as beer. Begun by Peter Reynolds, these courses are presently conducted by Peter Townsend and Vagi Frank — a key man in the records department of the personnel division.

The in-house South Pacific training courses were eventually held in a number of centres throughout PNG. External courses, too, were offered. The company Training Section developed correspondence courses in many general education subjects, both full and part-time. A total of sixty-nine persons were under training at 30 September, 1968, and in the annual report to shareholders, J.I.Cromie claimed with justifiable pride that South Pacific was setting an example to private enterprise in PNG.

Year by year, the South Pacific training effort was increased. In 1976, a typical year, seventy-eight Papua New Guineans were being trained, either formally or on-the-job in engineering, science, accountancy and business administration.

Inevitably, there were disappointments. The wastage rate, particularly in the earlier years, was high. Many young Papua New Guineans, unaccustomed to sustained mental application and with poor study habits, dropped out. Some left South Pacific after completing their training for other employers, lured by small increases in salary. The first student to be sponsored by the company at the University of Papua New Guinea — in 1970 — failed to complete his course. These are problems that, to a certain

Below *SP's Lae Brewery.*

Above *Peter Townsend, Group Training and Development Manager.*
Above right *Bill Fallon and (from left) Udia Seri, Patrick Nataloga, Gearson Kalula and Nicholas Thoran.*

Below *Vagi Frank, Industrial Relations Manager.*

extent, remain.

Results in the field of apprenticeship training, where as we have seen South Pacific was an early participant, were often gratifying. In 1968, Henry Onsa, a refrigeration apprentice, won the title of Apprentice of the Year, the top PNG award.

The refrigeration trade is naturally of critical importance to any brewery, and apprentices were lucky that the refrigeration manager of the company for many years — from March, 1967, to December, 1981 — was W.R. Fallon. An expert refrigeration engineer, Bill Fallon had a flair for training. Each of the four South Pacific sales regions today has a national refrigeration supervisor. Each — Patrick Natalogo, Nick Wambu, Horace Doti, Cleatus Keponge — came up through apprenticeship, and was personally trained by Fallon to a high standard of competence. Each has had the benefit of additional experience with Malayan Breweries, at Singapore or Kuala Lumpur.

By mid-1973, the company had thirteen apprentices under indenture, and was employing sixteen national tradesmen, plus a tradesman-fitter, who had completed a four-year mechanical engineering course. Ron Percival, currently in charge of apprenticeship training, joined the company in 1977. A fitter-machinist by trade, Percival was an ex-Navy man with experience at HMAS *Narooma* — the apprenticeship training establishment — and with the Department of Education in PNG. This background admirably equipped him to handle the apprenticeship programme, which in the thirtieth year of South Pacific's existence, 1981, was producing national apprentices and tradesmen capable of filling many technical and trade positions within the company.

'Our apprentices today come from the high schools,' Ron Percival told the author in January, 1982. 'They have a much better chance of succeeding than earlier apprentices. They complete form four, then apply for entrance into Pre-Employment Technical Training, or PETT. They do a full-time

Above *Leri Karukunu, Technical Training Officer, and (far right) with apprentices, at the Port Moresby Brewery.*

Below *Ron Percival, Senior Personnel Officer.*

course, twenty or forty weeks, in the trades they want to take on. Then they are eligible to enter into an apprenticeship.

'I worked out the actual programme for apprentices in 1977 with Bruce Preston, Bruce Flynn, Dave Longlands and Werner Bensch. Our biggest year was 1981. We had thirty-nine apprentices, doing fitting and machining, plumbing, carpentry, joinery, automotive, diesel, refrigeration, sign writing — even clerical, for the first time. At the moment we have twenty-four apprentices.

'Since I've been here, we've had some exceptional apprentices. Two were nominated in two successive years for the Apprentice of the Year short list — John Niva, a fitter-machinist, and John Toluarana, a welder. We have at present an exceptional apprentice in an electrical trade; Michael Ellison. We'll be nominating him for Apprentice of the Year, in 1982. His final marks in the PETT block course were 98 per cent electrical theory, 96 per cent electrical practice, 94 per cent allied subjects. Perfect English, and a good personality. He's going to Unitech, Lae this year, doing the Certificate of Electrical Engineering — our first apprenctice in electrical trades to do this course. We have five fitter apprentices who have gone through mechanical engineering. John Niva is doing exceptionally well. Leri Karukuru, my protegé who'll take over as training engineer when I go, was one of those who got their Certificate of Mechanical Engineering. He started as an apprentice...'.

Leri Karukuru, from Miaru village, Gulf Province, received his primary schooling in his village before attending Hohola Demonstration School, and Kila Kila High School. From an early age, interested in the technical trades, Leri went on to Moresby Technical College where he completed forms three and four, graduating in 1974. In January, 1975, he joined South Pacific as an apprentice fitter-machinist.

'Our training facilities then were not very good,' Leri told the author. 'But we worked hard, and today we have new buildings, new machines, new

131

equipment and a better training system as well. We are training apprentices to take over positions in different departments. I have been understudying Ron Percival since 1979, and when he goes I'll be in charge of engineering training for South Pacific apprentices. South Pacific is the only company I have worked for.'

There are a number of Papua New Guineans who have advanced through the South Pacific training system to satisfying positions with the company. From the time of the MBL-Heineken takeover, selected expatriate staff of South Pacific were given the opportunity of improving their knowledge and qualifications by periods of training overseas, principally in Australia, Malaysia, Singapore and Holland, and in more recent times the same chance has been afforded to national employees. Thus, in 1980 twelve attended overseas study and training courses. Among these were Kelly Riroriro, Leka Wari, Lavaki Susuve, Lesly Kidoro, Patrick Francis, Palsi Toa, Vali David and David Nelson. Their careers well illustrate the oppor-

Above *Leslie Kidoro, Personnel Manager, Lae.*
Right *John Peguero (centre) with brewers Leka Wari (left) and Palsi Toa checking beer for colour clarity.*

Below *Kelly Riroriro, brewer, Port Moresby.*

tunities that are available to educated Papua New Guineans with South Pacific Brewery Ltd.

Patrick Francis, who is one of the two national brewers in charge of different departments at Lae Brewery — the other is Changal Pankial — spent twelve weeks in 1980 at the Heineken Brewery, in Holland. He has worked in Singapore, too, with Malayan Breweries. Lesly Kidoro completed twenty weeks with Tooths and Castlemaine Breweries in Australia, and with Lavaki Susuve has attended the International Training Institute (previously Australian School of Pacific Administration) in Sydney. The veteran ex-District Commissioner and lecturer at ITI, Fred Kaad, has greatly assisted South Pacific (and other) students over the years, obtaining temporary positions for them with Sydney breweries and thus broadening their range of experience.

Kelly Riroriro, Leka Wari and Palsi Toa are brewers, in charge of

Above *Bob Robertson, Regional Manager, Highlands.*
Right *Arenu Kone (left) and Willie Moses, Statisticians.*

Below *Lavaki Susuve, Training Co-ordinator.*

various departments of the Port Moresby brewery under the direction of brewmaster, John Peguero. Peguero, a New Zealander, joined South Pacific in 1975 as a trainee brewer, after obtaining the degree of Bachelor of Technology at Palmerston North University. In 1976 he was sent to Singapore and Malaysia for further experience, and later to Holland and the United States. Born in 1952, John Peguero is young enough to appreciate and understand the problems facing Kelly, Leka and Palsi as they struggle to master their profession.

Kelly Riroriro comes from a little village in Collingwood Bay, in the Northern Province. From 1962 to 1968 he attended primary school at Popondetta, and then went to Martyrs Memorial High School, where he obtained his fourth form certificate in 1972. In 1973 he won a government scholarship to study science at the University of PNG, graduating with a bachelor's degree in 1977. He joined South Pacific Brewery in November of that year.

Since then, Kelly Riroriro has been thoroughly trained in various sections of the production department, and was sent to Malayan Breweries in 1979. He has since acted as supervisor in the packaging department, and in the brewhouse and cellars.

Leka Wari, from Hood Lagoon, obtained his secondary education at Kwikila High School. He graduated in 1966, and obtained a position as laboratory assistant at the Port Moresby brewery. Three year's hard study was rewarded by a promotion to manager of the laboratory, following which he was sent to Lae. For three more years he attended Lae Technical College, gaining his laboratory assistant's Certificate. He went overseas, to Singapore, in 1972 and to Holland in 1980. He then transferred back to Port Moresby, where he is currently supervising the brewhouse and cellars.

Palsi Toa, from Karkar Island, gained his secondary education at Tusbab and Sogeri High Schools, and graduated in 1978 as a Bachelor of

Robert Wato, signwriter.

Granso Barnabas, Port Moresby
Area Manager.

Science (food technology) from the University of Technology at Lae. He was sponsored by South Pacific in his final university year. His training with South Pacific followed along similar lines as the programmes developed for Kelly Riroriro and Leka Wari; a thorough study of the whole brewing process, overseas experience, more specialised work in the laboratory, and the bottling and canning areas.

Vali David has trod another path. Most of the young men understudying management and technical positions in South Pacific Brewery have had no other employment experience, having joined the company during or immediately after the completion of their formal education. Vali David has a different background. Educated at the Salvation Army Primary School, Koki, and Kila Kila High School, he joined the staff of the then House of Assembly in 1971, as a trainee interpreter. A self-taught musician, he played guitar in a local band in his spare time, and soon found this an all-absorbing interest. He left the House of Assembly in 1974, and accepted a position with Keynote Music House as a trainee piano tuner.

Determined to improve his knowledge of music, Vali David was one of twenty-five candidates — he was the only one from the Pacific Islands — who sat for the entrance exam for the Sydney Conservatorium of Music in 1975. The top six candidates were accepted. Vali was number seven.

Returning to Keynote, Vali David became a member of the very popular Clockwork Orange band. In September, 1976, he left the music house to work for South Pacific as a sales representatives in the marketing division.

'I went out on the road,' Vali told the author in December, 1981. 'It was very, very interesting, meeting different people, club managers and not hotel proprietors. I did a sixteen-week course in the brewery first, and later a couple of management seminars here in Port Moresby, run by the PNG Institute of Management and the Jaycees, as well as one held by the Australian Institute of Management in Sydney. I also did a course on business correspondence. I was four or five years on the road, and then Ken Webb suggested I look at a different role in South Pacific, rather than sales. He thought I'd be more suited to marketing and planning. That's what I'm doing now — understudying the national sales promotion manager, Bruce Parkes. South Pacific have looked after me. They are a good crowd to work with.'

Among Vali David's national colleagues in the marketing division are Enoch Toiai, Simon Tokias, and Granso Barnabus. Granso's father was once the house servant of Lloyd Ilett, who worked for South Pacific in the early days. These are young men on the way up.

One Papua New Guinean has reached the top with South Pacific — David Simon Nelson, from Balmo village, East Sepik Province. Born in October, 1952, David was the son of ex-Sergeant Simon Kurugumun, of the New Guinea Police Force and Royal Papua New Guinea Constabulary. David performed brilliantly at school — for four years running he was dux

Girls of the Port Moresby Brewery office staff. (Top, left to right) Marisa Kaerai, Olive Tabua, Hemyln Ila, Kara Morea, Bernadett Chakumai, Derry Willie. (Bottom, left to right) Regina Lillywhite, Mitty Toa, Imorea Sariman, Leva Bingeding, Loa Arua.

of Brandei High School — and in 1976 graduated from the University of PNG as a Bachelor of Arts, majoring in economics. He entered the PNG Defence Force as a commissioned officer, but was soon discontented, finding that he was not putting his degree to worthwhile use. Noticing a newspaper advertisement for a 'company secretary in training' for South Pacific Brewery, he applied, and was accepted, in January, 1977.

Ron Corden, the South Pacific company secretary, laid out a rigorous schedule for David Nelson, covering all aspects of the job. After two years of hard practical training, David applied for, and was granted, a scholarship under a New Zealand-PNG aid scheme to study for his diploma in business administration at Canterbury University. At the same time and on the advice of Ron Corden, he commenced a correspondence course to enable him to sit for the examinations of the Institute of Chartered Secretaries and Administrators, London.

Bruce Parkes and Vali David.

John Strong (left) Brewery Manager, and Patrick Francis, brewer, Lae Brewery.

David Nelson graduated with such distinction from Canterbury that he was offered a further two-year course to complete a master's degree in business administration at Massey University. During his three years in New Zealand, David was accompanied by his wife and four children. The New Zealand government paid his tuition fees and gave him a small allowance. South Pacific Brewery Ltd. made up this amount to his full salary, paid all accommodation costs and provided all books required.

David Nelson obtained his degree with first-class honours, majoring in finance and human resource management. He returned with his family to PNG in November, 1981. He has continued correspondence studies for the Institute of Chartered Secretaries and Administrators exams, and in 1981 topped a course of 7,000 students throughout Australia in company secretarial practice.

Clearly, few young men, regardless of nationality, have the ability and potential of David Nelson. On his return to PNG, he began further in-house training under the close direction of Ron Corden, with particular emphasis on accounting, legal, audit and computer functions.

At the suggestion of Corden, South Pacific had earlier introduced modern TELEX communications, and in June, 1979, leased an NCR 8250 computer, to cope with the greatly increased flow of business in the middle and late 1970s. The financial year of the company was also changed, to end on 30 September. South Pacific had been advised that National Provident Fund legislation would soon be passed which would further complicate the work of all company secretaries. It was necessary for David Nelson to be thoroughly familiar with these developments.

(In May, 1982, following the resignation and departure from PNG of Ron Corden, David Nelson was formally confirmed into the important, and demanding, position of Company Secretary of South Pacific Brewery Ltd.)

Space does not permit a mention of all the Papua New Guineans who

Neil Robinson, Regional Manager and (left) Geoff Nogo, Area Manager, Lae Brewery.

Above *Bruce Flynn, O.B.E., General Manager of South Pacific Brewery, and (right) Mea Morea.*

have contributed to the success of South Pacific. Women like the late Mrs Buruka Morea and her daughter, Mea, who is currently secretary-in-training to Bruce Flynn. The company secretarial and typing services were fully localised by 1974. Men like old Mosi, who established the beautiful gardens that help to make the Lae Brewery one of the most physically attractive in the Heineken Group empire. Peter Barnanga, Transport and Shipping Co-ordinator at Port Moresby, trained by Ralph Trundell and Brian Edwards. Giau Duruba, office administrator at Lae. Chauka Chakumai, works accountant at Port Moresby, and Suru Simon, assistant accountant. Chauka, a graduate of the University of Papua New Guinea, and Suru have received specialist training in Singapore, Malaysia and Australia.

Such training does not come cheaply. The total cost of training David Nelson exceeded K30,000. An estimated K15,000 has been spent on Chauka Chakumai. These are typical figures. The training budget of South Pacific in 1980/81 was K376,000, a considerable sum by any standard. But the company willingly accepts such costs, for its ultimate goal is the localisation of all positions in South Pacific Brewery Ltd.

138

14

Problems and Prospects

The major reorganisation of the South Pacific marketing operation along the lines suggested in the 1977 P.A.Management Services report had the desired result. By the end the 1970s, the market penetration of the rival San Miguel brewery had been contained, and reversed. The South Pacific share of the market improved from 78.1 per cent in 1977/78 to 85.2 per cent in 1980/81. A major triumph was scored in March, 1980, when South Pacific won first prize and a gold medal for its lager at the BREWEX Exhibition in Birmingham, United Kingdom, in open competition with the finest products of fifty-five breweries in thirty-eight countries. This was a great morale-booster for SP men. Production and quality control of the winning lager was carried out by brewmaster John Peguero, brewers Kelly Riroriro and Chris Speke, technological controller John Dickie and chemist Sape Sarevella. The gold medal was received on behalf of South Pacific by Patrick Francis and Leka Wari, who were at the time attending a training course with Heineken in Holland.

On 30 September, 1980, James Irwin Cromie retired, after twenty-nine years association with South Pacific Brewery Ltd. as director and chairman. 'A Grand Old Man Steps Down,' read a report in the *Post-Courier*, and it was an apt tribute. An outstandingly successful businessman and investor — a director of W.R.Carpenter Ltd. and for twenty-seven years chairman of Harvey Trinder Ltd. (now Bain Dawes) among other interests — Jim Cromie had also been a long-time supporter of both Anglican and Catholic Missions in PNG. He was succeeded as chairman of South Pacific Holdings Ltd. by J.H.G.Guest, O.B.E.

John Guest, an Australian company director and barrister, won his O.B.E while serving in the RAAF from 1940 to 1946. He left the Air Force at the rank of Wing Commander and began a distinguished career as a businessman. Among the many leading companies with which he has been associated as chairman or director are Mercantile and General Life Reassurance Company of Australia Ltd., Arnott's Biscuits Pty. Ltd., John

James Irwin Cromie.

139

Right *The Brewex Gold Medal Award in the hands of John Dickie, Technological Controller, with Leka Wari (left) and Patrick Francis.*
Below *Sape Sarevella, Scientific Officer, Port Moresby Brewery.*

Swire and Sons Pty. Ltd., Nicholas International Ltd., and Gibbs Bright and Company Pty. Ltd. This wealth of experience made his appointment as chairman a fortunate one for South Pacific.

There had been a number of other changes in the management structure of South Pacific. Some long-serving employees like Karl Thoennes and Rudi Bertram, engineer Werner Bensch and sales representative Roy McKain left PNG. Old hand Iluka Waru retired at the same time as McKain. It was the custom at South Pacific to recognise long-serving employees — national and expatriate — by the presentation of certificates and medals, the latter going to those completing fifteen, twenty and twenty-five years with the company. A presentation was made towards the end of 1980 to a group who had between them served South Pacific for more than 500 years, a striking testimony to the excellent relations that have always existed between the company and its employees.

Right *(Left to right) Chris Speke, John Peguero and Roland Kekedo, toasting SP's winning of the Brewex Gold Medal at the Brewery Exhibition, Birmingham, United Kingdom, 1980.*

At the retirement dinner for J. I. Cromie (from left) Rita Flynn, Jim Cromie, Bruce Flynn, Delphine Cromie.

Bertie Heath finally retired in April, 1980, at the age of eighty-seven. He was given a tremendous send-off, attended not only by everybody in South Pacific Brewery, but also by pilots from a later era in PNG flying, like Captains Bill Johns and Dick Glassey of Air Niugini.

The Board of South Pacific had changed little since the appointment of W.W.Gawne in 1973. Donald McKay was appointed a director in 1978, as an additional representative of Malayan Breweries Ltd., but resigned in October, 1981. J.H.G.Guest became a director in February, 1980. Among the alternate directors appointed was another Papua New Guinean, V. Navuru, as alternate for John Natera. Bruce Flynn was appointed a director in 1981.

Adrian Murphy was promoted to the position of assistant general manager of South Pacific on 12 September, 1979. Shortly afterwards, Rob Jackson, a young Scottish bio-chemist with a science degree from Heriot-

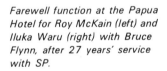

Farewell function at the Papua Hotel for Roy McKain (left) and Iluka Waru (right) with Bruce Flynn, after 27 years' service with SP.

Watt University, Edinburgh, and an extensive background of experience in English, Scottish and Welsh breweries and in cider manufacturing, became manager of the Lae Brewery. John Strong was by this time production manager at Lae.

Moresby Bottle Co. headquarters had been located for a long time at Lae, the major centre of SP production. The manager of this subsidiary company, New Zealander Eddie Wilkinson, joined South Pacific in 1966. Bottle recovery was still an important operation. New bottles, manufactured by the Australian Consolidated Industries factory in Lae, cost K2.60 per carton of twenty-four stubbies. Throughout PNG, some 5 million bottles of SP beer are sold each year. The cash replacement value of these bottles is clearly very high.

Under the direction of Eddie Wilkinson, some 300 full and part-time contract bottle collectors throughout PNG recover 70 to 75 per cent of all

Opposite page The prize-winning product.

Below *Bertie Heath, at the opening of Air Niugini House, July 1, 1977, with the Prime Minister, the Right Honorable Michael Somare (left) and the Governor-General, His Excellency Sir Tore Lokoloko.*

Above right *Farewell function given to Bertie Heath who retired from SP at the age of 87, after 20 years of service: (from left) D. Douglas, T. Alberton, P. Barnanga, B. Heath, F. Hammond, W. Pearson, D. Glassie, A. Preo, D. Williams, J. Dunstan, Capt. B. Johns, Capt. C. Gray, and M. Webb, son of SP's Group Marketing Controller.*

Right *Directors of SP: (from left) J.D.R. Neil, B. Flynn O.B.E., S. Iava, J. Guest O.B.E., D. Nelson, W. Gawne, L. Hurrell, C.M.G.*

GRASS ROOTS

MASSHKI WARI DALIN... MI LUKAUTIM YU IA.....

Don't worry darling . . . . . I'll look after you . . . . .

University of PNG female students yesterday called for a temporary halt to the sale and use of alcohol on the Waigani campus.

bottles sold. They are collected by Papua New Guinean collectors from the farthest locations — the islands, the coasts and the interior, even from remote Ok Tedi, site of PNG's ambitious new copper and gold mining project, where SP products are distributed through the nationally-owned Cloudlands Investment group. The empties are flown from Ok Tedi to Kiunga on the Fly River, and thence travel by river and sea to Port Moresby, where Moresby Bottle Co. continues to operate.

Bougainville Beverages has gone from strength to strength, under the management of Bruce Rohrshiem and sales manager Dick Thurgood. A major effort was made to upgrade the quality of the soft drinks — including Pepsi-Cola, manufactured under franchise — produced by Bougainville Beverages. Packing was improved, and rip-top caps introduced. Bougainville Beverages now commands approximately 98 per cent of the island's soft drink market.

Trading conditions in many countries of the world have been affected by escalating costs over recent years, and PNG is no exception. Beer excise was increased in both the 1980 and 1981 PNG budgets. The price of manpower and training continually rises, as do housing and maintenance costs. The National Provident Fund, which came into effect on 1 July, 1981, caused an immediate 7 per cent increase in employee-related costs. The Fund requires compulsory contributions based on 12 per cent of wage earnings, 7 per cent paid by the employer and the balance by the employee.

Power charges have risen dramatically. As well as being expensive, power supplies in major centres of PNG - particularly Port Moresby — have become so unreliable that most companies have been forced to purchase their own generators. South Pacific installed a powerful generator at the Port Moresby brewery in June, 1980, at a cost of K100,000. So essential has this generator become to the continuing operation of the brewery that two have been ordered for Lae.

Companies operating in major centres in PNG — and again, particularly in Port Moresby — face another employee-related cost that companies in Australia do not have to cope with — at least, not on the same scale — the security of homes and property.

House breaking has become a fact of life in PNG. The problem is most acute in the nation's capital, Port Moresby, where the South Pacific headquarters are located. It has become necessary for South Pacific, and other companies, to spend heavily on security protection, not only for its many business premises, but also for employee accommodation. Nobody — Papua New Guinean or expatriate — is immune from the gangs of 'rascals' who roam the streets of Port Moresby after dark, and the police, short of money, manpower and equipment, have been unable to contain their activities.

Urban house breaking, and related offences, are of course only an aspect of the deteriorating law and order situation in PNG noted in chapter ten. It is unfortunately true, too, that alcohol abuse continues to plague the nation.

144

GRASH ROOTSH

EH... NOKEN RAUSS-SSHHIM BLARY HA.. HA.. HALIKOHOL IA... NOGGATT!!... EM BUN BILONG YUMI SSHTRET...

Hey.... you can't ban bloody alcohol..... no Sir..... it's our real strength.

Chimbu's three-month liquor ban had the support of a vast majority of people in the province, Premier Matthew Siune said yesterday.

The most casual examination of the newspapers since the South Pacific education programme, 'Operation Moderation', was forced to a halt, confirms this.

Bureau of Statistics figures issued in November, 1978, indicated that over the eight years from June, 1970, the annual consumption of beer per head rose from 8.1 litres to 15.9 litres, an annual growth rate of 8.8 per cent. These figures indicate a very moderate rate of beer consumption in PNG by world standards, but do not reveal the fact that most alcohol consumption takes place in urban centres, and in the Highlands. Many Papua New Guineans do not drink beer, or do so only on occasion.

The number of licensed premises has increased very rapidly since the passing of a law in 1977 allowing the provincial governments to take over the liquor licensing function from the national government. The first to take advantage of these new powers was the Eastern Highlands Provincial Government. In August, 1977, this authority introduced a retail beer sales tax of forty-eight toea per carton sold within the province. The tax proved to be a bonanza for the provincial government, K66,000 being collected in the first three months. Other provinces quickly followed suit, introducing beer taxes ranging from forty toea to K1.20 per carton. Ten of the nineteen provincial governments had elected to take over the liquor licensing function by the end of 1981, and there seems little doubt that the number of licensed liquor outlets will continue to increase.

Over the past few years, concern over rising alcohol consumption rates in PNG has resulted in a number of attempted remedies, campaigns and inquiries. All kinds of solutions have been tried or proposed, but to little avail. Education programmes, licence freezes, liquor sales restrictions and bans, excise and price increases, trading hours restrictions and extensions, increased police activity, lower alcohol content (SP beer today has an alcohol content of 3.6 per cent by weight) — all have failed to check increasing alcohol consumption.

PNG has one of the highest motor vehicle death rates in the world, and a link between alcohol and fatal road accidents has been proven. The annual reports of the Royal Papua New Guinea Constabulary contain ample evidence of this, and are confirmed by independent studies. A vigorous anti-drink-drive campaign was launched in December, 1978, by the Department of Transport and Civil Aviation. The message, 'Don't Drink and Drive' was rammed home in newspaper advertisements, on theatre screens and on radio, but the effect, unfortunately, was limited. Despite recommendations by the 1971 Committee of Inquiry, no action has been taken to assist police to control drink-driving by the use of breathalysers.

Savage tribal fighting in parts of the Highlands continues to the present day. The causes are many but are usually connected with conflicting land claims. Alcohol undoubtedly fuels some Highlands conflicts. Desperate measures have been resorted to by the national and provincial governments, apart from such milder actions as liquor trading restrictions and bans, to

145

Above *Product display featuring the Gold Medal (foreground) won at the International Lager Competition against 75 entries out of 55 breweries from 38 countries.*
Right *John Nilkare, Minister for Decentralization, at SP's Special Draught launch, at SP Lae Gardens, October, 1980.*

Above *A mobile bar at Port Moresby waiting to be loaded onto the* Hiri Chief *for shipment to Kiunga. The bar will be one of three used as canteens in the Ok Tedi mining venture.*
Right *25 years of service awards presented by Bruce Flynn to (from left) Karl Thoennes, Veva Kii, and Nesti Singalong.*

Right *The four original Port Moresby hostesses (from left) Marjorie Mark, Stephanie Nakat, Kevani Seneka and Mary Wilson.*

GRASS ROOTS

H HEM NAU... HI'LL DRINK TO THAT...

MI TU... BURP..

Alcohol abuse is threatening the health, welfare, safety and national development in PNG, according to a report released yesterday.

control tribal fighting. Over the past few years 'Fight Zones', suspending certain civil liberties and giving the police extra powers, have been declared in various Highlands regions — and once, to its shame, in the city of Lae and environments — and in July, 1979, Prime Minister Somare took the unprecedented step of declaring a State of Emergency in the five Highlands Provinces. This, the most extreme action any government can take short of a declaration of martial law, followed a bloody series of raids and pay-backs that had left thirty-five tribesmen dead and over 200 wounded during the preceding six months. Tribal fighting was checked, but resumed after the emergency period expired.

In June, 1980, it was reported that the crime rate in Port Moresby was up by 55 per cent compared with 1979. The then new Prime Minister, Sir Julius Chan, declared a war against crime. He reported to Parliament that the murder rate in PNG was soaring — 138 cases in the 1979/80 financial year. New Fight Zones were declared in Enga and Southern Highlands Provinces at the end of 1980.

And so the cycle continues. It would be idle to deny that the abuse of alcohol has played a part in the law and order problems that bedevil Papua New Guinea. But only a part. The problem is too complex, with too many facets, to be explained away by merely throwing the total blame on alcohol.

The liquor industry has continued to provide much needed funds for the government of PNG, and employment for its citizens. During the ten years from July, 1972, to September, 1981, South Pacific Holdings made a total net profit before tax of K17,585,000. During this decade, excise collected by South Pacific and paid to the government amounted to K128,531,600. Another K5,690,035 was paid in company tax. South Pacific, too, collects the retail beer sales tax on behalf of the various provincial governments — a task that had proven beyond them.

The continuing reliance of the PNG Government on the liquor industry for the generation of funds was indicated early in 1979, when the government announced that it was seeking overseas investors for a multi-kina hotel development at Ela Beach, adjoining the Davara Hotel. Early in 1980, negotiations were successfully concluded with the big Indian group, Oberoi Hotels International, to undertake the project. In March, Oberoi released details of its proposal to build a 300-room, international standard hotel on the Ela Beach site, at a total cost of K20 million. At least 25 per cent of the equity will be held by Papua New Guinean shareholders. It was then estimated that the hotel would be open for business at the end of 1984.

In mid-1979, a World Health Organisation expert, Dr Gerald Milner, made a four-month visit to PNG to inquire into problems associated with alcohol, on behalf of the National Liquor Licensing Commission. In a submission to the inquiry, South Pacific Brewery Ltd. noted that the brewing industry in PNG directly employed 1,000 people, with an employment multiplier effect of at least ten to one — an overall direct and indirect

IR JULIUS...
UT OL I RAUSIM
ELA LIKA BAN
IS IA... EM BAI
ARAPIM MIPELA
ETA LONG
IN...

EM NAU...NOGUT
OL I BIHAINIM
TINGTING BILONG
YU... EM BAI
BAGARAPIM
MIPELA LONG
BUS
TU...

YESIA.. NA
EM BAI BAGAR-
APIM MI LONG
BLA RY POKET
BILONG MI
STRET!

KAWAG
BILAK
MAKET
PTY LTD
FOR NEVER
ENDING
SUPPLY

Hey..... Sir Julius..... they'd better not cancel this liquor ban business..... it's really going to ruin us town people..... That's true.... it's no good if they follow your idea..... that will mess up us bush people too.....
Yes Sir..... and it's going to really hurt me right in the pocket.

a six month ban on take-away beer in the High-lands could force people to buy beer from blackmarke-teers .
"It will force them to go outside the law. It will encourage people to sell at ex-orbitant prices. It may even instill in the minds of the people an 'alcohol cult'."

employment of around 11,000. This was a guess estimate only insofar as the indirect employment aspect was concerned, but was in line with the conclusion reached by the government economist, W.R.Irlam, in 1971, and referred to in chapter eight of this book.

On 1 January, 1980, the PNG Institute of Applied Social and Economic Research (IASER) commenced an alcohol research programme on behalf of the Ministry of Justice, then under Mrs Nahau Rooney, MP. This is a continuing programme. On 15 October, 1981, a number of policy rec-ommendations were made by the IASER research team to the national and provincial governments of PNG.

The IASER team concluded that PNG was 'presently poised on the brink of serious major social and health problems related to alcohol abuse'. The best way to reduce alcohol consumption in PNG was to limit its avail-ability, and the first body of recommendations related to this objective. Other recommendations were concerned with the need for the development of educational and informative programmes; the need to reduce the road toll by the use of breathalysers and the introduction of a stiff driver/blood alcohol-level law, and the establishment of an independent statutory govern-ment body, to be called the PNG Alcohol and Drug Abuse Research Centre. This Centre would prepare education programmes, establish and operate alcohol and drug abuse centres and treatment programmes, and collect vital statistics.

Whether or not the IASER recommendations will be implemented in whole or in part is, of course, a matter for the government of PNG to decide. Impartial observers would certainly agree that a thorough government-sponsored educational campaign on the evils of alcohol abuse is long overdue. This is the view of South Pacific. Whatever is decided, South Pacific Brewery will continue to abide by the policy laid down by the government.

15

`Operation Armada´

On the eve of South Pacific's thirtieth anniversary year, an event of great significance to Papua New Guinea took place: the Third South Pacific Festival of Arts held in Port Moresby and other centres from 30 June to 12 July, 1980. It was the first time that the Festival had been held in PNG.

The Festival brought to PNG, representatives from countries all over the Pacific; New Hebrides, American Samoa, Western Samoa, Marshall Islands, Kiribati, Tuvalu, Niue, New Zealand, Cook Islands, Australia, Federated States of Micronesia, Tahiti, Guam, Solomon Islands, Hawaii, Northern Marianas, Nauru, New Caledonia, Palau, Wallis and Futuna Islands, Tonga and Fiji. Dancing groups, artists, instrumentalists and craftsmen came together in what was described by Don Stewart, Deputy Secretary-General of the South Pacific Commission, as 'the most spectacular and biggest assembly of art and culture' ever held in the Pacific Region.

By common consent, the highlight of the opening of the Third South Pacific Festival of Arts was 'Operation Armada', a magnificent descent on Ela Beach of a mighty fleet of gaily decorated, heavily manned canoes, watched by over 20,000 excited spectators — a stunning opening to the Festival, and an event never before staged.

'Operation Armada' was planned, organised and funded by South Pacific Brewery Limited.

The project had its beginning in 1979, when initial proposals for the Festival were being examined. One evening, the South Pacific Brewery group marketing controller, Ken Webb, was in his car, returning home after a function in the VIP Room at the brewery. He turned on the car radio to catch the news broadcast, and heard for the first time that the South Pacific Festival of Arts was to be held in PNG in 1980.

A keen marketing man, Webb was immediately struck by the fact that the brewery and the Festival shared the same name. 'I could see right away that here was a big event that we could assist with our nation-wide distribution setup,' Ken Webb told the author when recalling the time. 'We

Racing towards Ela Beach.

151

could help the Festival organisers to get their message across to the PNG the Festival organisers to get their message across to the PNG people, and at the same time the company might get some good public relations mileage out of it. We're always prepared to put some money into projects that will help PNG without looking for a direct return, but after all, we do sell beer!

'I knew Mali Voi, from the National Cultural Council at Waigani, who was one of the main Festival organisers. I had a meeting with Mali and offered our help. Over the next few months Maureen MacKenzie and Arts School students developed the Festival logo, featuring a carved crocodile head against a decorative circular background. We incorporated it into a beautiful set of beer coasters, advertising the Festival. We commissioned a Melbourne artist to do the design, and we also used it on Festival posters which we distributed to licenced premises all over the country. So we gave the Festival a big publicity boost long before it happened.

'Mali Voi was appointed Director of the Festival and the late David Bamford was his deputy, while Bart Philemon was Chairman of the Board of Governors. By the time detailed planning began, we were in constant touch with Mali. At one meeting Mali mentioned that the Manus people were going to send two traditional ocean-going canoes on the 1,900-kilometre voyage to Port Moresby, to join in the celebrations. We all got pretty excited about this, and out of our discussions came the idea of expanding this voyage by two canoes, into an Armada, pulling in canoes from all the maritime districts and maybe even from other Pacific countries. I don't remember whose idea it was — it might have been Mali's, or David Bamford's. We decided there and then to go on with it.'

SOUTH PACIFIC FESTIVAL OF ARTS

PAPUA NEW GUINEA 1980

At this time, Gerry Faramus was advertising manager of South Pacific, following the retirement of Roy McKain. He was the logical choice to run the Armada project, for he was an experienced yachtsman, secretary-manager of the Royal Papua Yacht Club for six years prior to joining the company, and he had a good personal knowledge of the Papuan coastline. Gerry Faramus was appointed Armada Co-ordinator.

The problems facing Faramus were formidable. He had no precedents to guide him, but he was given a free hand and the promise of sufficient funds and assistance to do the job in style.

'The first thing I had to do was try and work out an estimate of the total number of canoes and people we could expect to take part,' Faramus told the author in January, 1982. 'Then I could work out a budget to take to Ken Webb and Bruce Flynn. I did a preliminary trip around the coastal and island provinces as the first step, handing out 500 special posters and publicity material to provincial government officers, teachers and so on, and to all of our own depots. Then I did a second trip, to see who was interested in joining the Armada. I got a very positive response and I estimated that up to 600 canoes would be in the fleet, each with a crew of at least six. So that would be about 3,600 people we'd have to look after. All my planning from then on was based on that figure, although the final numbers in the Armada

152

Right *A.J. Murphy, former Assistant General Manager of SP, presenting SP's donation cheque to Bart Philemon, Chairman of the South Pacific Festival of Arts.*
Below *Gerry Faramus, 'Armada Co-ordinator.'*

were much less.

'How were we going to feed, water and sleep so many, and look after their safety? It would be too dangerous to sail canoes after dark along that reef-strewn coastline, so overnight stops were going to be required. I decided to make Mullins Harbour, near Samarai, the first rendezvous point. The two Manus canoes would join us there, plus about 100 others from outlying districts. Then we would sail along the Papuan coast in stages of six to eight hours, stopping overnight at Kupere, Abau, Gavuone, Hula, Gaba Gaba and then the final overnight stop before Port Moresby, at Tupusereia. Other canoes would join the Armada as we sailed along.

'A real headache was trying to work out how to get food to each overnight stop. There's no coastal road past Kupiano. We finally used trucks where we could, and then ships and aircraft. We arranged with the local people at each stop to supply fresh foods and water, for which we would

pay. We provided things like meat, tea, sugar, chickens, toilet rolls, rice and biscuits. And it all had to be delivered at just the right time. Too soon, and the fresh meat and frozen chickens would rot — they don't have refrigerators out in the villages! Too late, and the Armada would have sailed on.

'The planning went on for months before the event. As time went by there was a feeling of hesitation among the coastal tribes. They were doubting whether the Armada would ever sail — the whole project was becoming too much for them to comprehend. So a fortnight before the start, I had to do another field trip to reassure them.

'All this was costing South Pacific a packet. I was chartering ships, aircraft and helicopters, buying meat, rice and all the rest of it, and there always seemed to be more things needed. When I worked out my initial budget, I reckoned I could do it all for about K10,000. But costs — particularly travel and transport costs — went on rising, and I had to go back to

154

...... *the course, Port Moresby. (Photos by A. Zable).*

Ken and Bruce Flynn and ask for another K10,000. "OK," they said, "but not a toea more!". But it still wasn't enough — the final bill for direct costs came to about K50,000.

'My final food bill alone was pretty frightening. We ended up buying nearly 2,000 kilograms of fresh beef plus ten cases of canned meat, 200 frozen chickens, 225 kilograms of pork, 300 kilograms of fish, 650 of rice, 17 bags of sugar, 53 kilograms of tea and all sorts of minor things. And we paid out a lot of money at the overnight stops.

'Of course, there were a hell of a lot of people involved apart from me. Just about everyone in South Pacific was in it at one time or another, particularly Bill Fallon, Ralph Trundell, Tala Hobart, Vali David, Emmanuel Lei, Ted Momo, Siniwa Sili, Laga Kala and Dave Longlands. Jack Nuoai and Jack Lahui of the Hiri Canoe Association were in it early on, and they helped us to find area co-ordinators at the overnight stops — John Wala, our own refrigeration mechanic Gearson, Pat Ila, Walo Karo, Jack Nuari. The Defence Force boys helped a lot, particularly Francis Molean and Bob Dadimo, who kept in touch with the Defence Force escort vessel and the two Manus canoes throughout their tremendous voyage. Each of the canoes carried Defence Force navigators and radio operators.

'Kipling Gombo, the Civil Defence director, provided rescue boats and transceivers. The officers-in-charge of the government stations along the coast — Andrew Kogare, John Ine, Francis Nianfop, Same Joke — were of great assistance. Greg Hoskins, John Nilkare, Gideon Zebulan and a lot of councillors and schoolteachers all helped. Col Garland of Standard Telephones and Cables looked after the public address system at the finishing point, Ela Beach. There were lots of others who gave us a hand.

'Our final action plan ran to twelve foolscap pages, and looked like an Army logistics exercise, which it practically was. Disaster struck just as the

Below *The Gogodala and their 30 metre racing canoe. (Photo by T. Cooke).*
Bottom *The Armada leaves Tubusereia village. (Photo by T. Cooke).*

ship carrying the bulk of the food for the overnight stops was about to sail. The wharfies went out on strike, and tied up Port Moresby! I went to the union and pleaded with them. We had to get that food out, or the Armada would be a flop. They agreed to let our ship, the *Kuku*, sail but no other. Then we got word of a drought along the coast, so we had to send out eight truckloads of water in drums, plus firewood for the earth ovens.

'As Armada co-ordinator, I was to sail with the canoe fleet from Mullins Harbour. I went in a supply truck to Kupiano. Just in case, we made up a huge barbecue plate in the South Pacific workshop, and carried it in the back. It was an enormous thing, about fifteen by twenty feet, and it was so heavy that it took fifteen men to lift it. It had a cooking capacity of about 500 steaks. Just as well we made it — we used it half a dozen times at least.

'We left Moresby on 21 June for Kupiano, and next day a helicopter came in with Graham Dimmett as passenger, and we flew to Mullins

Harbour. Graham was making a video film of the entire event.

'We arrived at Mullins Harbour, expecting to find eighty or a hundred canoes assembled, and to my horror I couldn't see a single one! I said to the pilot, "This can't be Mullins Harbour. We must be in the wrong place!" But it was the harbour, all right. I thought to myself, "My God, this is going to be a washout, and I've spent about K50,000 of the company's money". Then I spotted a solitary canoe. It was the little *Velevelago*, from Milne Bay. Some Armada!

'Things soon improved, though. Our escort ship, *Marie Louise*, was there as planned, with spare fuel, extra rations and so on, and the rescue launch I was to travel in. The support vessels outnumbered the Armada! But we had to leave, with the *Velevelago* as the sole official starter.

'On 24 June we found the two big Manus canoes at Amazon Bay. They had sailed nearly 2,000 kilometres without any trouble. Then a Suau canoe

The welcoming at Marshall Lagoon.

Left *Leaving Abau Island.*

Left and right *The morning of the last day. (Photos by A. Zable).*

arrived, with four exhausted crewmen. Next morning we were about to move off when we were joined by another thirteen canoes, and I began to cheer up.

'We got a fabulous reception at Abau, a huge feast, people everywhere and more canoes waiting to join the fleet. On we went, and the fleet got bigger every day. All our arrangements worked perfectly. I was in regular contact by radio with Civil Defence in Port Moresby, and the NBC reporter on the escort vessel sent reports each day on our progress, which the NBC broadcasted. Film and video units caught it all too, from aircraft and helicopters.

'The people at each stop seemed to be competing with each other in their hospitality. Thousands at every stop — it was really something.

'By the time we reached Tupusureia, the fleet was more than 150 strong. It was bedlam. We were so close to Moresby that visitors and tourists came out in droves, and a lot of the food we provided for the Armada crews went down the wrong throats. There was dancing and singing and noise — aeroplanes and helicopters overhead — all very exciting. We did not have the 600 canoes we hoped for, but it was still the biggest fleet ever seen in these waters.

'The big day dawned, Monday 30 June. I was up before dawn to check the winds and weather. We had to hit Ela Beach at 10 a.m. sharp, when the Prime Minister and VIP's would be arriving. A hundred and fifty crews had to be fed, and a hundred and fifty canoes rigged and held until it was time to go. I was afraid they'd get all excited and start racing and spoil the mass arrival we'd planned for so long, so I went ahead in the launch to set the pace. We left Tupusereia at 8 a.m.

'I looked back at the fleet behind me, and it was a phenomenal sight. The canoes were all built of traditional materials, except for the sails. Most of these were made of nylon, in all the colours of the rainbow. It was a beautiful, sparkling morning, with a blue sky and a good stiff breeze, and that great mass of canoes was just fantastic.

'On the way to Ela Beach we were joined by a canoe from the New Hebrides, and then a huge Gogodala racing canoe from Western Province, with crews fifteen strong. West New Britain canoes turned up, and a horde of locals from Elevala, Poreporena, Porebada, and Tanobada. I gave the Armada their heads off Local Island, and there were probably 300 in the fleet by then. Off they raced for Ela Beach. The wind was right and they simply flew. They hit the beach almost exactly on target, a few minutes past ten, before a cheering, clapping, laughing crowd of more than 20,000 people, many of them from other Pacific countries, and other parts of the world.

'It was a hell of a big effort and it left me pretty exhausted, but it was something I'll remember for the rest of my life.'

It was, indeed, a marvellous opening to the Third South Pacific Festival of Arts. The final cost to South Pacific Brewery was somewhere between

Opposite *At the helm. (Photo by A. Zable).*

160

The Armada arrived at Ela Beach just after ten in the morning, before a crowd of over 20,000 spectators.

Above *A commemoration medal was presented to all participants of the Armada.* Right *The commemorative stamp issue.*

K75,000 and K100,000. A medallion, specially minted by the company was presented to each Armada crewman. The Manus people reciprocated with a large model of one of the superb ocean-going canoes that had made the long voyage to Port Moresby, which was given the place of honour in the South Pacific Brewery VIP Room.

An unexpected, but very welcome, public relations bonus for South Pacific Brewery was the issue by the Philatelic Bureau of Posts and Telegraphs of a commemorative stamp issue to mark the occasion of the Festival. Each stamp bore the legend, 'S.P. Festival of Arts'!

16

The Road Ahead

South Pacific Brewery Ltd., thirty years on, faces the next thirty years with confidence in its future in a strong and prosperous Papua New Guinea.

The three decades of the company's existence have seen the advance of Papua New Guinea from colony to independent State. Problems aplenty were faced and overcome by the new nation in the process; problems aplenty remain and they, too, will be overcome.

Few would deny that Papua New Guinea has managed the transition to independence more happily than most of the new nations of what has come to be known as the Third World. Few would doubt that it is the destiny of Papua New Guinea to become a leader among the island nations of the Pacific.

South Pacific Brewery, too, intends to maintain its position as the leader of the brewing industry in Papua New Guinea. Vigorous competiton has always been a feature of the liquor industry, and certainly the fight in the marketplace between South Pacific and its rival, San Mig, has been fierce in recent times. Competition is the life-blood of successful enterprise, and the struggle between the breweries continues.

As market leader, South Pacific does not intend to rest on its laurels. The superior quality of the product has been amply proven by its success in international competition, and in 1982 the company launched an export drive, concentrating on a fine new premium beer packed in cans bearing a splendid label featuring PNG's national bird, the bird-of-paradise. Designed by Cato Hibberd, one of the world's top packaging designers, the new label is both striking and colourful.

In June, 1982, the company proudly announced the first major export order for the new SP Special Export beer. Two container-loads (3,180 cartons) were sold by the South Pacific selling agent in Hawaii, Larry Graff, to Primo Distributing Company Inc., a major liquor distributing organisation. This sale followed a number of market-assessment visits to Hawaii and the West Coast of USA by Ken Webb and Special Projects Manager, Bruce Parkes. Intensive efforts to develop further export markets are continuing.

SP Hostesses at the launching of the Special Export Lager, 27 May, 1983 (from left) June Lee, Ligori Gorogo, Judith Kuschell.

165

Opposite page *The SP Export Lager can (top, far left) and the launch function in Honolulu to commemorate the export of SP Lager to the United States.*
Above *Kubulon Los (centre), Papua New Guinea's Ambassador to the United States, at the Honolulu launch, with him is Ralph Wari, a PNG student attending the University of Hawaii.*

The list of South Pacific shareholders today is small, as the major parcels are still held by Pacific Holdings Ltd., the Public Officers Super-annuation Board, and the Defence Force Retirement Benefits Board. A few of the original shareholders' names appear on the list, however; strong links with the past — Cecil Showman, Meg Ashton, Ira Halliday, Bill Seale, Bill de Rusett, Gwen Wylie and Nell Bergstrand.

The company policy of South Pacific Brewery, formulated many years ago, will continue to guide the company along the road into the future.

'To comply in letter and spirit with laws and regulations and co-operate with the Government; to help strengthen the economy of Papua New Guinea and the well-being of her people, employing local goods and services wherever possible; to employ, train and develop personnel, building and maintaining a loyal and efficient staff devoted to the better-ment of Papua New Guinea, Company and Self; to be a good citizen and neighbour, observing all local customs and practices and developing an understanding of, and interest in, the welfare of the community and its people; to produce the highest quality beer, developed by constant research, always zealously guarding the reputation of our trade mark, and to aid the development of the industry by supplying our product at a fair price.'

167

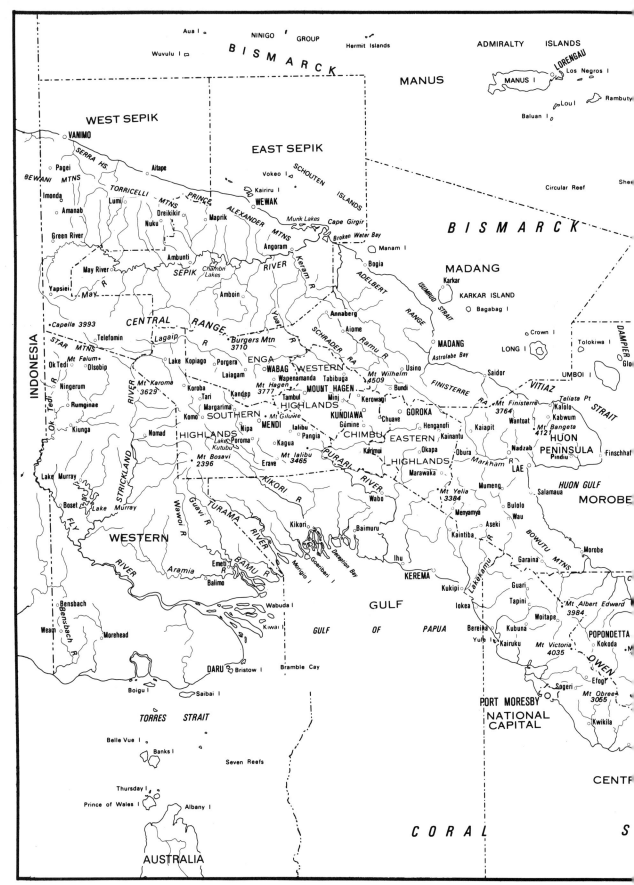

BISMARCK

NINIGO GROUP
Aua I
Wuvulu I
Hermit Islands

ADMIRALTY ISLANDS
MANUS
LORENGAU
MANUS I
Los Negros I
Lou I
Rambuty
Baluan I

WEST SEPIK
VANIMO
SERRA HS
Pagei
Aitape
EAST SEPIK
Vokeo I
SCHOUTEN
BEWANI MTNS
Imonda
TORRICELLI
Kairiru I
WEWAK
ISLANDS
Circular Reef
She
Amanab
Lumi
MTNS
Dreikikir
Maprik
Munik Lakes
Cape Girgir
BISMARCK
Green River
Nuku
PRINCE
ALEXANDER
MTNS
Broken Water Bay
Manam I
Ambunti
Angoram
Bogia
MADANG
Karkar
May River
Chambri
Lakes
ADELBERT
KARKAR ISLAND
Yapsiei
SEPIK
RIVER
Keram R
RANGE
Bagabag I
May R
Amboin
Capella 3993
Vual R
Annaberg
ISUMRUD STRAIT
CENTRAL
RANGE
Burgers Mtn
3710
Aiome
Ramu R
Crown I
LONG I
Tolokiwa I
Telefomin
Lagaip
SCHRADER RA
MADANG
UMBOI
Glo
STAR MTNS
R
ENGA
WESTERN
Usino
Astrolabe Bay
Saidor
DAMPIER
Mt Faium
Lake Kopiago
Porgera
WABAG
Mt Wilhelm
FINISTERRE
VITIAZ
Ok Tedi
Olsobip
Laiagam
4509
STRAIT
Ningerum
Koroba
Kandep
HIGHLANDS
Bundi
RA
Mt Finisterre
Teliata Pt
Mt Karome
Mt Hagen
MOUNT HAGEN
Kerowagi
3764
Kalolo
OK Tedi R
3629
Tari
3777
Tambul
Minj
Kabwum
Rumginae
Margarima
Komo
SOUTHERN
Mt Giluwe
KUNDIAWA
Chuave
GOROKA
Wantoat
Mt Bangeta
4121
HUON
Kiunga
Nipa
MENDI
Ialibu
Gumine
Henganofi
Kaiapit
PENINSULA
Nomad
HIGHLANDS
Pangia
CHIMBU
EASTERN
Kainantu
Nadzab
Finschhaf
Lake
Poroma
Kagua
Karimui
Obura
Pindiu
Mt Bosavi
Kutubu
Mt Ialibu
PURARI
HIGHLANDS
Markham R
LAE
Lake Murray
2396
Erave
3465
RIVER
Marawaka
HUON GULF
STRICKLAND
Wabo
Mumeng
Salamaua
MOROBE
Boset
KIKORI R
Mt Yelia
3384
Bulolo
FLY
Lake Murray
Guavi R
TURAMA
Baimuru
Menyamya
Wau
Kikori
Aseki
BOWUTU MTNS
Morobe
WESTERN
RIVER
Ihu
Kaintiba
Garaina
RIVER
Aramia
Emeti
Morigio I
Goaribari I
Deception Bay
KEREMA
Guari
LAKAKAMU
Balimo
BAMU R
Tapini
Mt Albert Edward
Bensbach
Wabuda I
GULF
Kukipi
3984
Bensbach R
Kiwai I
OF
Iokea
Woitape
POPONDETTA
Wean
Morehead
GULF
PAPUA
Bereina
Kubuna
Kokoda
Yule I
Kairuku
Mt Victoria
OWEN
DARU
Bristow I
Bramble Cay
4035
Boigu I
Saibai I
Sogeri
Mt Obree
3055
Efogi
TORRES STRAIT
PORT MORESBY
NATIONAL
Belle Vue I
CAPITAL
Kwikila
Banks I
Seven Reefs
Thursday I
Prince of Wales I
Albany I
CORAL S
AUSTRALIA

168

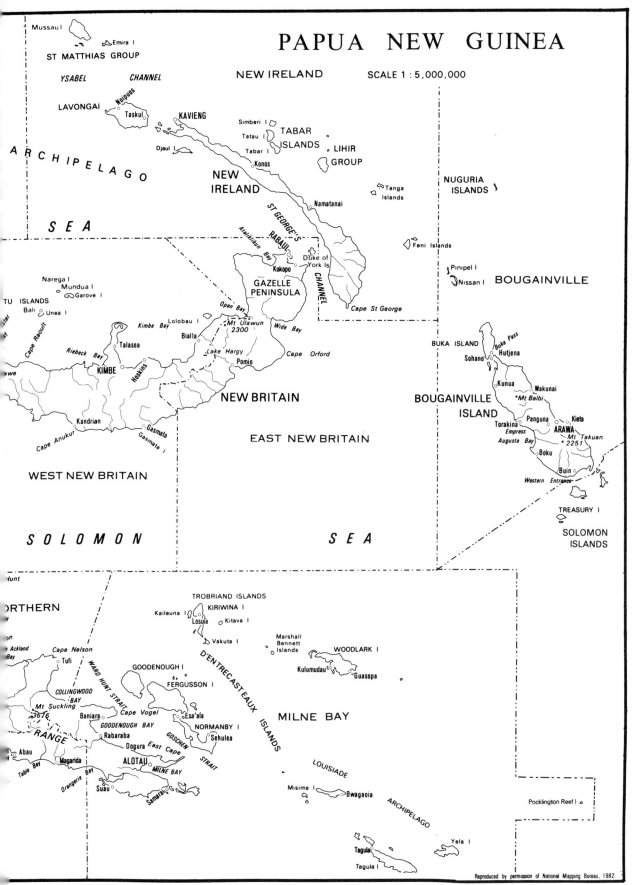

PAPUA NEW GUINEA

SCALE 1 : 5,000,000

Mussau I

ST MATTHIAS GROUP

Emira I

YSABEL CHANNEL

NEW IRELAND

LAVONGAI

Noipuos

Taskul

KAVIENG

Djaul

Simberi I

Tatau I

TABAR

Tabar I

ISLANDS

LIHIR

GROUP

A R C H I P E L A G O

Konos

NEW
IRELAND

NUGURIA
ISLANDS

S E A

ST GEORGE'S

Ataliklikun Bay

RABAUL

Tanga
Islands

Namatanai

Narega I

Mundua I

Garove I

TU ISLANDS

Bali

Unea I

GAZELLE
PENINSULA

Duke of
York Is

Kokopo

CHANNEL

Feni Islands

Pinipel I

Nissan I

BOUGAINVILLE

Cape St George

Open Bay

Mt Ulawun
2300

Lolobau I

Kimbe Bay

Wide Bay

BUKA ISLAND

Buka Pass

Cape Raoult

Riebeck Bay

Talasea

Bialla

Lake Hargy

Pomio

Cape Orford

Sohano

Hutjena

we

Haskins

KIMBE

Kunua

Wakunai

Mt Balbi

Kandrian

Gasmata

BOUGAINVILLE
ISLAND

Panguna

Kieta

Cape Anukur

Gasmata I

NEW BRITAIN

EAST NEW BRITAIN

Torakina

Empress
Augusta Bay

ARAWA

Mt Takuan
2251

Boku

WEST NEW BRITAIN

Buin

Western Entrance

S O L O M O N

S E A

TREASURY I

SOLOMON
ISLANDS

Hunt

RTHERN

Ackland
Bay

Cape Nelson

Tufi

TROBRIAND ISLANDS

Kaileuna

KIRIWINA I

Losuia

Kitava

GOODENOUGH I

Vakuta I

Marshall
Bennett
Islands

WOODLARK I

COLLINGWOOD
BAY

Mt Suckling
3676

Baniara

FERGUSSON I

Kulumudau

Guasopa

Cape Vogel

Esa'ala

D'ENTRECASTEAUX ISLANDS

MILNE BAY

RANGE

GOODENOUGH BAY

Rabaraba

NORMANBY I

Sehulea

Dogura

East Cape

GOSCHEN STRAIT

Abau

Magarida

ALOTAU

Table Bay

MILNE BAY

LOUISIADE

Orangerie Bay

Suau

Samarai

ARCHIPELAGO

Misima I

Bwagaoia

Pocklington Reef I

Yela I

Tagula

Tagula I

Reproduced by permission of National Mapping Bureau, 1982

169

Opposite *A display of products relating to the new Special Export Lager.*

Epilogue: As this book was going to press, it was announced that on February 2, 1983, South Pacific Holdings had made an offer for all the ordinary shares in San Miguel (PNG) Limited of seven toea per share, an offer which the major shareholder, Neptunia (PNG) Proprietary Limited, holding 91.4 per cent of San Miguel ordinary shares, advised it would accept.

In a joint statement, the Chairman of South Pacific Holdings and the Chairman of San Miguel (PNG) Limited said, that the merging of the operations of the two breweries would rationalise production and distribution of both ranges of beers within Papua New Guinea. Bruce Flynn gave an assurance that Papua New Guinean staff of San Miguel would be re-trained, retained or re-deployed where needed, and that the policy of sponsoring sport, community effort and supporting Papua New Guinean-owned businesses through South Pacific and San Miguel Management Services, would be continued.

Index